Teaching to Observe

The Counselor as Teacher

By

Jay E. Adams

TIMELESS TEXTS
Woodruff, SC

CONTENTS

Preface

In my *Christian Counselor's Commentary* on James 3:1 I urged someone to write a book dealing with the matter of teaching in counseling. I have decided to heed my own exhortation. I hope that the publication of this text will initiate a line of thinking that, in time, will lead to more specialized material explicating in depth various aspects of the subject that I shall here explore in general.

When I say that, however, I do not want to be misunderstood. I do not wish to leave the impression that the material here is abstract, consisting of mere principles and propositions. Rather, I have tried to make this volume a practical handbook to which the busy, practicing counselor may turn for guidance and help. Indeed, one goal I have in view in writing is to provide a text for training purposes. I hope that this book will provide help for the education of Christian counselors that, to my knowledge, does not yet exist. Yet, on the other hand, nothing is more practical or necessary than principles rightly applied. Principles cover large areas of thought and activity, as specific rules do not. So I have tried to base all the practices that I advocate squarely on biblical presuppositions and principles.

In speaking about additional material yet to be written, what I am trying to say is that some things contained in a book like this, that covers the waterfront, can be treated elsewhere in more depth as a series of volumes. The matters covered generally here may have specialized aspects that need further explication for various situations and in unique circumstances. Moreover, there may be a deepening of material upon which here I have only begun to comment. I hope to provide hints along the way for those who would follow after.

Well, be that as it may. Why write *Teaching to Observe (The Counselor as Teacher)*? I have two main objectives in doing so.

In writing for counselors (and counselors-in-training) I hope (1) to convince those who may not have given much thought to the matter that teaching is an integral part of counseling, and (2) to give helpful guidance and instruction to both novices and seasoned counselors about how to teach in the counseling context.

I have been counseling since the early 60's, have dealt with hundreds of people (perhaps thousands by now—I have lost track), and have rarely been involved in a counseling case in which some sort of teaching was not necessary. In the course of such extensive counseling, I have learned something about teaching. What I have learned, and think is important, I want to leave with you as a legacy.

With reference to the first objective that I mentioned above, it is necessary to observe that Carl Rogers spent most of his adult life attempting to persuade counselors that teaching during counseling should be taboo. His perspective on the matter, widely propagated and accepted, was that because man is essentially good, at the core of his being he has all of the answers he needs prepackaged within. That is why, in his view, good counseling is evocative rather than educative in nature. Indeed, his tenets were so strict in this matter that he taught his followers to be careful about the manner in which they elicit information from the counselee, lest even the tone of their words, gestures or facial expressions might "teach" or convey something to the counselee. Once, addressing a group of teachers, he went so far as to tell them that true teaching was not possible.

Consequently, Rogers developed a reflective model of counseling in which, by means of a stereotypical manner, he hoped to reduce even this unwonted, incidental "teaching" to a minimum. He recognized the essentially contradictory nature of his efforts: dogmatically teaching ways to avoid teaching! He banned anything that might tend to "lead" the counselee's thinking by even a mildly Socratic method. The counselor must neither guide nor hint; he must be acutely aware of the danger of indirectly doing so. Even questioning—if not reflective in nature—would be wrong. He must restrict his words to repeating ("reflecting") the content of the counselee's comments. Thus, according to Rogers, the counselor himself became little more than a mirror.

Many persons over a wide variety of disciplines, as a whole or in part, accepted this view. That they were always as careful not to "teach" (even incidentally) is questionable. But to this day you will hear people using Rogerian stock phrases—"I see that you are torn two ways," "What I hear you saying is...," etc. And there are many who when they talk about counseling speak of it essentially as "listening." Because so many have been influenced, consciously and unconsciously, by this view of counseling which, at one time, was a prevailing system in America, much residue (if not outright adoption) of Rogerianism still may be found in counseling circles. Thankfully, Rogerianism is dying, but we must reckon with the fact that it is dying hard!

Since Rogerians do not believe in inculcating the views of others in counselees and, therefore, strongly oppose teaching in counseling, it is necessary to make a case for teaching among those who have suffered from the baneful effects of Rogerian fallout. It is even necessary to convince many counselors that, contrary to Rogerian teaching, teaching in counseling is a vital part of the process.

The second purpose in view in the writing of this book is to provide a broad coverage of the place and methods of teaching as these pertain to counseling. There are many books about teaching, and a plethora about counseling, but, to my knowledge, none about the place of teaching *in* counseling. It is time to address and remedy this situation.

Jay E. Adams
Enoree, South Carolina
1995

Chapter One

Does Counseling Require Teaching?

When I speak of counseling, I mean (of course) *biblical* counseling. I am not going to argue the case for biblical counseling since I have done so elsewhere—indeed, in numerous places. Rather, I shall assume that the reader is a genuine Christian, one who trusts Jesus Christ as the Savior Who died for his sins and rose again from the dead. In other words, I shall presuppose that the reader believes the gospel (found, for instance, in I Corinthians 15:1-4). Moreover, because I am writing to believers, I shall assume that you—my reader—*want* to be biblical in your counseling. That that is a large assumption, I realize, but for the sake of brevity I shall nonetheless make it.

I *cannot* assume, however, that you entirely buy into the nouthetic counseling movement (for information on this movement and the meaning of nouthetic counseling, see my book *Competent to Counsel*). That would be assuming far too much. I think, therefore, that it is only proper to warn you that agreement with the material in this book will serve to make you more nouthetic in your counseling (directive counseling and teaching in counseling are close cousins). But even counselors who claim not to be nouthetic, I hope will profit from the book.

Since I do not believe neutrality possible in anything that we think, say or do, I am unable (and, I might add, unwilling) to attempt to divorce myself from my beliefs as I write. It would be hypocritical and foolish to do so, and of greater importance, lack of loyalty to Jesus Christ. So, what you will encounter in the

1

pages that follow is a nouthetic approach to teaching in counseling. Indeed, the very idea of teaching in counseling *is nouthetic.*

I must demonstrate biblically that teaching is an essential
part of counseling. Until the days of Carl Rogers, who almost
single-handedly trashed the age-long definition of the word
counsel by persuading a generation of counselors that counseling is not a matter of *giving counsel or advice* but, rather, a particular brand of listening, people all knew what counsel is. He
converted many so-called "counselors" into mere *listeners.*
Those who adopted Rogerian principles and practices were no
more counselors than ballet dancers are. Whatever else they may
have done in the name of counseling, they simply *did not counsel.* The idea of giving counsel or advice was a central taboo in
Rogerian thought.

It must be taken as an axiom that the biblical words for counsel (*tachbuloth, maam, yeam, etsah, rigmah, yaats, sod* in
Hebrew, and *boule, sumboulion, nouthesia* and, sometimes, *par-
aklesis* in Greek), all of which in one way or another mean "giving advice" or "giving guidance and direction," are definitive of
God's view of counseling. While I do not intend to milk these
terms, this fact alone is an important matter that should be kept
in mind as we continue.

Never, in the Bible (or in any other literature prior to Rogers)
was counseling equated with or defined as a process designed to
change a counselee by eliciting information and direction solely
from the "counselee," apart from input by his "counselor." In all
biblical uses of the terms for counseling, as in previous non-bib-
lical uses, the infusion of a counselor's advice into the counseling process is, as a matter of fact, *primary.*

The task of a counselor, *as counselor,* always has been to
counsel, i.e., to offer guidance, instruction and advice. The counselor is approached by others in order to elicit his opinion, to
obtain information and to gain from deliberation something that
the counselee could not have known or determined otherwise.

There are times when a good counselor is called on even to admonish or rebuke. Change in the counselee, leading to a lifestyle pleasing to Jesus Christ, is the *purpose* for engaging in Christian counseling. Thus counseling involves giving and receiving biblical instruction from a scripturally knowledgeable counselor who is able to evaluate the counselee's situation according to biblical values and is able to locate, explain and apply biblical teaching to that situation so that the counselee's lifestyle may more perfectly approximate one that honors Christ. Of course, none of this implies that the counselee is passive. For teaching to be profitable, the counselee must evaluate, learn and otherwise appropriate what he is taught. But for change to accord with the Bible, when not already known, much must be *taught*.

Good counselors confront the counselee in his situation, guide him into interpreting that situation in the light of the Bible, and through direction, encouragement, and monitoring his progress, help him to make whatever changes God requires. All of that is implied in the biblical terms already mentioned and the contexts in which they are used. I do not intend to enter into study of passages in which these terms are employed, but any who doubt my analysis of the biblical data in this regard should themselves do so. They will find that, without exception, the biblical terms for counsel *all* imply data and input to be given by the counselor. If that is true, Rogerian thinking is wrong. If that is true, counseling must involve teaching. To fail to teach when necessary, then, is to counsel ineffectively.

It is not surprising that the need for teaching in counseling should be challenged. This is the latest ploy of the evil one by which even some Christians (and clergy) have been duped. While turning counseling into reflective listening is a modern twist, it is just that—a new twist of an old theme. From the Garden of Eden it has been Satan's purpose to challenge the truth of God's Word. If he can convince would-be counselors not to use

that Word at all, so much the better! It is by God's Word that
man, from his creation, has been linked to God. In the Garden,
the devil asked history's first question—a question about the
Word of God: "Has God said...?" His intention? To raise *doubt*
about God's command. Moving on further, he then *distorted*
God's Word: "Has God said that you may not eat of the trees of
the Garden?" God told them that they may eat of all of the trees
except the tree in the midst of the garden—the tree of the knowledge of good and evil. Finally, following doubt and distortion
came outright *denial*: "You will not die." He attacked the facts in
the Word, then the veracity of the Word of God Itself.

From the beginning, then, the dissemination of doubt, distortion and denial of God's Word has been Satan's standard M.O.
To find him at it again, attacking God's Word, in a slightly different way, should not surprise us. His latest strategy is to *dis-
count* the need for God's Word while at the same time to
displace the Word with human opinions gleaned from ignorance
and sinful thinking. Above all else, it seems, Satan hates God's
Word and seeks in every way possible to supplant it with his
own. Alert biblical counselors are aware of his wiles.

Does man need a Word from God? Yes! On two counts. In
creation, before the fall, man was utterly dependent upon God's
Word for data about his purpose and place in this world. Nor did
he know how to go about achieving the goal of his creation apart
from that Word. The dominion mandate and the fruitfulness
command, by which man was taught and commissioned to
occupy and control the earth, were necessary for this end. God
was his Instructor and Interpreter. Man did not come prepackaged with all the knowledge he needed to conduct his life on
earth. He was absolutely dependent on God for this information.
That which tied him to God was His Word. It was Satan's purpose to break the tie by attacking and destroying the link God
forged between man and Himself. So he directed all his efforts
toward the Word of God.

The second reason that man needs a Word from God is the fall. After man's fall into sin it became even more necessary for him to have a Word from God. The link must be reestablished not only to discover meaning and purpose but to restore proper relations with God. In his sinful rebellion, man exchanged the truth of God for the devil's lies (Romans 1:25). He opened his mind and heart to the misleading counsel of the ungodly (see Psalm 1) and lost true knowledge as he defaced the image of God. Today, apart from the message of good news and the regenerating power of the Spirit that enables him to believe and follow it, man is lost. He must have the knowledge of God "renewed" (restored) by receiving, understanding and obeying God's written Word (cf. Colossians 3:10). Even a Christian cannot find his way in this world apart from God's Word. That is why counselors must assume the role of teachers of the Word of God as a significant part of their counseling.

To summarize, it is because at creation man was constituted as a being who was dependent on God's Word for direction, meaning and purpose, and because subsequently he exchanged the Father of Lights for the father of lies, that advice-giving in counseling, as indeed in all ministry, is essential. And it is for these two reasons that this teaching must be based entirely on God's Word, the Scriptures of the Old and New Testaments in which form the Word of God has come to us. Man *as man* and man *as sinner* needs God's Word.

In addition to this, one must not suppose that man is a *tabula rasa*, a blank slate. He is born with a nature that is oriented away from God and from truth and readily accepts error and engages in sin. Therefore, in counseling, the Christian is faced not only with the task of pointing toward and teaching truth but must also contend with and displace falsehood. As a teacher, he is faced with the task of replacing error with true knowledge. Since the Christian counselor must advise counselees, he must have an authoritative Source of knowledge from which he draws that advice. That knowledge should be gleaned from the Bible and he should (increasingly) be in possession of a fund of knowledge and wisdom that is at his fingertips and on the tip of his tongue, ready to be dispensed as needed. If that ultimate source is not God's Word, what will it be? If he draws from some other fountain, what will make his advice distinctively Christian? If it is not truth from God that he dispenses in teaching, how can he justify his counsel as authoritative, or even as legitimate? Who has the right (not to say gall) to counsel another about his life problems and issues if he does not have an authoritative Word from God by which he is commanded and taught to do so? If it is but the counselor's word, or the word of some other sinful man that he dispenses, there is no reason for the counselee to heed his advice. After all, the Christian counselee knows enough to be aware of the fact that "all have sinned" and that, therefore, all have embraced error and—to a large extent—are void of truth.

The arrogance of counselors and others who say that their counsel, insight, direction and advice is correct and ought to be followed, on no firmer basis than their own say so (or the assurances of other sinful men who do), ought to be apparent. But you are a Christian counselor. Certainly you do not want to thrust your opinions and judgments into the lives of confused and (often) overly susceptible counselees. That is why you will endeavor to counsel entirely according to the Bible, God's sufficient Word.

Chapter Two

Your Sufficient Textbook

Is God's Word sufficient for counseling and teaching in counseling? As a Christian counselor you have a unique privilege among teachers: you possess an all-sufficient and absolutely correct Source of information from which to derive your teaching. As a matter of fact, this text is inerrant. And this information, found in the Bible, has been specially compiled in God's textbook format. We shall discuss the difference between that format and modern formats presently, but for now, this: you do not have to keep on buying new textbooks and discarding old ones as viewpoints change and knowledge increases; the textbook God gave you is unchanging and needs no revision because of better understanding. In its original form, it already contained all that is necessary for life and godliness—and that means it needs no replacement, supplementation or revision!

Scientific "knowledge," for instance, is in constant flux: medical and electronics textbooks are often outdated before they reach the reader. The same is true of nearly every field of human endeavor. But, rightly interpreted and applied, after millennia, the Scriptures prove as up to date and applicable to modern problems as if they were revealed last week. That is because, at bottom, sinful man has not changed. Nor has God!

The Bible does not become obsolete. It contains all that anyone could ever need to live a life of godliness in *every* age and culture. Because of this fact, and because the Bible is a true revelation from God the Creator, in all respects this—the Church's textbook for teaching in counseling—is *unique*.

"But is the Bible really a textbook for counseling?" someone asks. "After all, you don't use it as a textbook for nuclear science, for genetic engineering or hundreds of other disciplines. Then why counseling? What makes counseling—and teaching in counseling, in particular—so different?" Those are the sorts of questions that one encounters over and over again in the discussion of these matters. They deserve a solid answer.

You are correct in observing that the Bible is not a textbook for aerospace studies or automobile designing, etc., etc. But it is precisely because it is not those things that it *is* a textbook about what to teach in counseling. The Bible has a focus, and it is this directed focus that makes it a textbook for teaching God's will for man. God did not give us the Bible to make us more effective fishermen or draftsmen, but He *did* intend to make us more righteous persons through the message of the Bible. The *purpose* of the Bible (though because of the way in which some dismiss it for counseling you'd think that there was none) is to enable the lost to be saved and the saved to be sanctified. To make redeemed sinners godly is its stated purpose. And rightly used, it achieves that purpose. The Bible, to put it differently, was given to provide all the data, direction and drive necessary for one to be able to love God and love his neighbor (Matthew 22:36ff.).

The Bible deals with interpersonal relationships—exactly the content of counseling problems. It tells you how to relate properly to other persons in ways that glorify God. When counselees come for help, they don't expect you to help them repair a broken down automobile; but what they *do* need is to know how to repair broken relationships with God and their neighbors. Their concerns circle around children, spouses, parents, persons at work, relatives, themselves. Their concerns are about interpersonal matters. And *that* is what the Bible is all about. Since it deals definitively with interpersonal relationships, it is a counseling teacher's textbook.

Granted the format is not one you are used to. Its form does not correspond to modern textbook methodology. Yet it is God's sort of textbook, and therefore, when correctly understood and used, it is much more user-friendly than those that conform to modern methods. "Really?" you ask. "It seems to me that, if anything, it would be easier to study and understand and use if it were in modern encyclopedia or textbook form." Let's consider that objection for a minute or two.

Is the objection valid? Well, of course, if you had an encyclopedic list of items to which you could turn alphabetically, it would be easier to look up all that God has said on a subject. But would it be more useful? No. The format in which most biblical teaching is given is *truth applied.* Not only does God convey a truth, but He does so in the context of a situation in which that truth is applied. The Good Samaritan teaches you how to love your neighbor, the Rich Fool tells you how to provide for tomorrow. And so on. Once you have grasped the truth in the context of the parable, the story, the historical incident, you will forever be able to remember it and to recall how to apply it in life. Besides, how can you adequately explain love, mercy, grace, humility in an encyclopedic manner? Instead, it is much easier to understand what these concepts mean when you see them manifested in the story of the crucifixion of Jesus Christ. In other words, the application of truth (even in the case laws of the Old Testament) gives you something to which to attach truth so that you may understand and remember it better and (of particular interest to the counselor-teacher) shows you how to apply it to interpersonal problems concerning God and man.

God knew what He was doing when He gave us the Bible in the form in which He did. And once the counselor becomes used to using it in the manner in which it was given to be used, he will only have to agree. For more information on this issue, see my books *What to Do on Thursday* and *Truth Applied.* In these two volumes you will discover how to use the Bible as it is given to be used.

When Peter says that the Bible has all things necessary for life and godliness (II Peter 1:3) what that means is not that the Bible speaks directly to every issue that ever could be raised in counseling, but that in addition to many such direct comments, it provides principles that cover all. We may, therefore, distinguish between scripturally-directed commands, either in the form of individual directives or general principles, and scripturally-derived ones, developed from the former by good and necessary consequence (see the Westminster Confession of Faith, I:6). We are always to be absolutely sure about the former; sometimes, because human reasoning from principles and directives may prove faulty, we must be somewhat cautious about the latter. But even though the Bible does not speak directly about everything, it clearly sets forth *all* that is necessary to love God and one's neighbor *perfectly*—were one to follow it to the full.

Let's take an example of each in order to illustrate this distinction. It is not even doubtful, according to Exodus 21:10,11 that the three things necessary to constitute the willingness to continue a marriage on the part of the husband are his provision of food, clothing (or shelter) and sexual relations. That is stated in the passage. But it is by inference that the willingness of a woman to continue a marriage involves her acceptance of the first two provisions from her husband and her provision of sexual relations for his benefit. The first is a plain biblical directive; the latter, a biblically-derived principle that stems from the former.

There is, then, every reason for thinking that the teaching counselor will have more than enough information to impart to his counselee. Since there are other fine books dealing with the sufficiency of the Scriptures I shall not take the time here to retrace paths that you may travel elsewhere.

Chapter Three

But Should You Teach?

Should you ask, I can answer that question. The answer is *yes* and *no*. If you are a Christian, regenerated by the Holy Spirit, placing your faith in Jesus Christ as your Savior, *you should counsel*. In His Word God calls all of His children to an informal ministry of counseling. A number of passages attest to this. For instance, Paul writes to Christians in general, "you yourselves are full of goodness, filled with all knowledge, and competent to counsel one another" (Romans 15:14). And again, "Let Christ's Word dwell in you richly, as you teach and counsel yourselves as wisely as possible" (Colossians 3:16). Moreover, consider Galatians 6:1: "Brothers, even if a person is caught in some trespass, you who have the Spirit should restore him in the spirit of meekness." In all three of these verses, the average man (or woman) in the pew Christian is addressed. It is clear, then, that God expects all Christians to counsel. (In my two books *Competent to Counsel* and *Ready to Restore* you will find more complete developments of these verses.)

Like it or not, all Christians are called on to counsel; and that means to *teach* (indeed, the verse in Colossians specifically mentions teaching in the same breath: teaching is also linked with counseling in Colossians 1:28). Because biblical counseling necessarily involves teaching, it is important for every Christian to know God's Word so clearly that "it richly dwells within" him. He must be "filled with all knowledge" of it, and he must be "competent" to counsel fellow believers. Moreover, it is his obligation to become adept at giving "wise" counsel. And he must acquire what it takes to be able to "restore" erring brothers.

11

All of these connecting comments, in addition to the observation that faithful believers will be "teaching" one another (Colossians 3:16), indicate the need for obtaining knowledge and the ability to teach in counseling. Knowledge, wisdom, restoration, etc., all involve teaching.

As a part of the mutual ministry that is assigned to every believer, God expects you to be prepared to counsel fellow believers whenever it becomes necessary to do so. This is a part of the ministry that God ordained as a means for the church to build itself up in love (cf. Ephesians 4:11,12,16). The pastor-teacher of the flock is to equip all the saints for their work of ministry; that means that he must *train* his members in counseling (he may want to use this book as an aid). Everyone, therefore, should learn at least the fundamentals of Christian counseling, including knowledge about how to teach truth during sessions.

"But your answer was equivocal; you said, 'Yes and no.' What did you mean by that?" Simply this: while all Christians should counsel one another *informally,* unless called officially by God to the ministry of His Word and ordained by His church to the task, one should not take it upon himself to become a *Counselor.* It is one thing to counsel informally, as needs arise; it is quite another to set one's self up as a counselor. The latter is to be done only by those who have received this call from God and His church. Apropos to this matter, James wrote: "My brothers not many of you should become teachers, because you know that we teachers will receive greater judgment" (James 3:1). It is one thing to teach (or counsel); it is another to become a teach*er* or counsel*or.* It is this lawless sort of *self*-appointment to which James addresses his words, not to the informal, mutual ministry of teaching in counseling that should go on among the saints all the time. James is explicit regarding the matter: it is teachers like himself to which he is referring (cf. "we teachers").

"But James is talking about *teaching*," you reply, "not counseling." Precisely. That is my point. Even from the angle of teaching—as one aspect of counseling—the work of counseling as a formal life calling is restricted to a *few* (to use James' words, "not many of you"). These few are those whom God has called, especially equipped and set aside for that work. It is certainly not for all. Because counseling involves becoming a teacher and teaching, not everyone may take that task upon himself. Indeed, many who never should have done so have arrogated the position of counse*lor* to themselves. Consequently they are doing harm in Christ's church.

Let's consider that point. There are far too many (and by the same token, far too few) involved in counseling—as *counselors*. Many who should heed James' warning (and it is that) seem not even to know that it applies to them (perhaps largely because they fail to associate teaching with counseling). They attempt to counsel from an extremely shallow and/or meager understanding of revealed truth (that is, if they use the Scriptures at all!). Some, whose beliefs are quite erroneous or at points even border on the heretical, have little fear of the consequences of violating James' admonition. To counsel authoritatively, as a part of a life calling by God, is to be called to the work of the pastoral ministry and requires extensive, accurate understanding of the Word of God. One must know how to locate pertinent biblical passages, exegete them properly, apply them with precision and implement them practically. To acquire and develop these skills takes training, time, direction and discipline. And it requires a definitive calling from God. God's professional counselor is the pastor.

On the other hand, there are those who have the training, skills, abilities and call mentioned above who *fail* to counsel. And a number of them have developed more than adequate communication skills that they use in the pulpit. In short, they can teach and do teach regularly—except in counseling! Because they do not recognize counseling for what it is—an essential part of the ministry of the Word to which they were called (cf. Acts 20:20,31; Colossians 1:28)—they do not use these skills and abilities in counseling. Such ministers often have been brainwashed in seminaries into thinking that counseling ought to be done by others whose specialties are in psychology rather than in Bible.

Others have been frightened off of teaching by the charge that it isn't fair to teach counselees who, in a vulnerable state, might more easily accept their teaching in an uncritical way than at other times. What? Should Paul have not taught grieving Thessalonians facts about the second coming and the resurrection as he did (I Thessalonians 4:13ff.)? The notion is false, predicated on the idea that one teaches his (or another's) theory—not God's healing truth. What better to teach suffering saints than God's restoring and strengthening Word? Indeed, why not be grateful if problems make them more susceptible to it? As a matter of fact, in a dramatic statement that applies to how Jesus Himself learned, God says that suffering provides an ideal environment for some kinds of learning (Hebrews 5:8).

The effect of this anomalous situation, in which many who should don't teach, is that Christian counselees often receive poor counseling. If any is offered at all, the advice they are given may be inadequate or shoddy. They seldom are given detailed, accurate biblical teaching regarding their problems, and perhaps more frequently than one would like to think, they are directed or allowed without protest to take actions and make decisions that displease God. Persons ill-equipped to counsel attempt to do so, while those who are equipped doctrinally and otherwise do not. *This situation must not continue!*

Let's take a closer look at James' warning (and don't fail to notice that it *is* a warning). James warns the "brother" (the feminist NRSV shamelessly tampers with the biblical text by adding the words "and sisters" with absolutely no manuscript warrant) that "not many" should become "teachers." Why? Because, he says, teachers will be judged more strictly than those Christians who are not (literally, the Greek reads that they shall receive "greater judgment").

When God evaluates the life and efforts of those within the church who teach, He will overlook no aspects of their ministry. They have been (or have been failing in the work of) guiding and directing His people. That is of concern to Him. It is a serious matter to take upon one's self the position of a counselor to God's church (whether it be on a local, national or international level). God will not have His church mistaught and His people misguided with impunity. When the fires of judgment burn, many will be chagrined to discover how thoroughly the wood, hay and stubble that they used as building materials will be consumed. God wants those who build on the true and only foundation of Christ to "be careful how they build." If they do not "look" with care at what they build and how they build it, making sure that the materials they use are gold, silver and precious stones that can endure the fires of judgment, rather than receive a "reward," these builders will "suffer loss" (I Corinthians 3:10-15). Again, those words of Paul were written to *warn*.

So, in every way, false teaching (and teachers) are to go unheeded and must be eliminated from that position in the church (Romans 16:17; I Timothy 1:3,4; 6:20,21; Titus 1:10,11, etc.). Those who seek to build up the church must be "wise" builders. Psychological wood, hay and stubble cannot build the church. Only the precious metals and stones of God's revelation can do that. It is dangerous, therefore, for any Christian to take up counseling as a "job" or in a perfunctory manner. To give erroneous counsel or, because of inadequate knowledge of the Scriptures, to lead counselees astray cannot be looked upon as inconsequential—to either counselee or counselor.

Now surely neither James nor Paul in issuing their warnings intended to drive off for fear of failure those whom God has called to counsel. No one is perfect, no one possesses complete,

accurate knowledge and understanding of the Bible. But, as
James says, the number of full-time teachers in Christ's church
ought to be limited to those who have been called to the work
and who are diligently applying themselves to the task of learning as fully as possible what the Scriptures teach and how to
minister this truth to God's people.

There are broken marriages that are the result of failure to
heed the apostolic warnings. There are families dismembered
because erroneous psychological (rather than biblical) advice
was dispensed in the Name of Christ—and was followed. There
have been congregations rent asunder by pursuing courses of
action recommended by counselors who should have known better, but didn't. The situation today has grown acute. It is time for
these warnings to be trumpeted aloud in the church.

Another serious matter must be addressed. There are those
whose teachings for years have strongly influenced the church to
follow psychology and to avoid what they loved to call "simplistic" teachings of those who have dedicated themselves to counseling biblically. The views of biblical counselors who have
developed a systematic approach to counseling based on the
Bible have been pooh-poohed. One teacher, who has rejected
nouthetic counseling as so much "nothing buttery" (criticizing it
for using *nothing but* the Bible), on the tape of an address at
Moody Bible Institute's 1995 pastor's conference, recently con-
fessed that,

> I have had a hunch for years, as I dealt with people
> in my professional office that when I really helped it
> was not because of my professional expertise.

He went on to say,

> ...all these years I've never felt like an expert. I've
> always been waiting to be found out [laughter]. And
> I've done a rather good job, because I'm fairly ver-
> bal and I think reasonably well, of hiding behind jar-

gon and all sorts of impressions and expertise. I pretended. I don't want to pretend any more.

What an astounding confession of guilt! One wonders how many others are in the same boat. To know that what one is doing and teaching others to do is ineffective or wrong, yet to go on "pretending" that it is not, "hiding behind jargon," etc. (not to speak of the ethics of charging clients fees under false pretenses), in the light of James' and Paul's warnings not only must seem reprehensible but extremely dangerous. Surely Larry Crabb's followers will consider themselves betrayed! Imagine buying into a system that the founder eventually admits he knew was useless and that he continued only by pretense. That cannot happen to those who truly depend on the Word of God rather than supposed "expertise."

One can only hope that Crabb's present conversion to a more biblical approach in counseling may, in time, become complete. And one must also hope that this turnabout is genuine and not but another pretense driven by some other unspoken agenda. In the spirit of I Corinthians 13:7, however, unless events prove otherwise, I must take his word that his change is sincere, though after hearing him speak about "pretending" and "hiding" (I admit) the cynical side of me cannot but wonder.

Until adjustment of belief and methodology are complete, it would be wise for persons like Larry who have come to such new convictions not only to repudiate their former errors publicly, but to take adequate time to reformulate and recast their systems before they write or teach again. There is much to be changed (On the same tape he says, "I have been uncomfortable to some degree with just about everything I've been doing for the last twenty-five years"). Unless an Arabian desert experience like Paul's occurs, one fears that what will issue forth is but something else that may also contain error, but less visibly so, since it is the product of a laudable, but too hasty, attempt to become biblical. Declaring one's new beliefs scriptural too soon, when many of the psychological stains have not yet been laundered, could be even more devastating to those who buy into his latest scheme. It is possible that, like the past system that Larry is in the process of abandoning, the new one also may be *called* "Biblical Counseling" when it is not. Surely this new turn on his part does not involve a repudiation of truly biblical counseling, only of that which he once wrongly *called* biblical counseling. But that is just the point. He has in the past called his approach biblical; now, in rejecting it, he does not intend to reject biblical counseling. He must be rejecting that which he *falsely* called biblical. Unwittingly, the same can happen again if he is not careful.

Since I wrote those words, Crabb's article in the August 16, 1995 issue of *Christianity Today* has appeared, in which he writes, "...I feel like a ten-year old describing his wife. He hasn't met her yet; he's not quite sure what she's going to look like....At one level, I haven't got a clue what I'm doing. But I have a couple of central convictions, and I don't think I've ever felt more directly led by the Lord." By this admission, Crabb is unprepared for teaching. Yet, it seems, he is going to go on doing so. I urge him to wait. Be sure this time so that he will not have to pretend again. Much more than a "couple of central convictions" is needed for a teacher (especially one who views himself a teacher of teachers!). Paul would never have sallied forth with so little. And as for "feeling led"—there alone is a statement that should raise flags all over the place. The Bible nowhere indicates God leads by feelings.

Like Paul turning from Judaism, it will take time for Crabb, and others who truly put off the old ways, to put on the new ones. The fear is that when such individuals "come over" to true biblical counseling, it will be only a coming over *as they see it*, and not as it ought to be. Should Larry, or others like him, begin to write and lecture immediately, you must be wary of what they say; good intentions—no matter how sincerely meant—will not substitute for accurate exegesis, careful theological understanding and correct application to the lives of counselees. "Not many of you should be teachers" lest you find yourselves twenty-five years later repudiating what you have been saying all along. We welcome you Larry—and any others who want to move in the right direction. We will give all the help you may request. We are anxious to see you in the role of a sincere (no more pretending) and valiant member of the biblical counseling movement.

There is one more item. Part of having misled persons in the past (particularly when one has done so by "pretending" and "hiding behind jargon") is genuine **repentance**. Nothing less should be expected from one who confesses to such things. After all, he has taught error in counseling and taught others to do so as well, and in pretense and hiding. That is serious if James' admonition is to be understood. And repentance should lead to works appropriate to it. At the very least, those works flowing from repentance should cause one to demand of himself greater care about any new views he adopts and teaches, lest in more subtle ways he continue to wrongly influence believers to their detriment. Moreover, it should lead to a firm determination never to counsel or teach counseling in ways that lack the basic integrity of one's wholehearted belief that he is doing God's will. There is no place for pretense. To declare that one has turned to biblical counseling that is to be done through the officers of the church (elders), and then to do so without acquiring a *thorough* exegetical and theological understanding of the Bible's teaching about elders and shepherding, would be lamentable.

In the taped presentation, one regrets to say, there was not the slightest whisper about repentance. Indeed, some of the remarks were of a jocular sort, drawing laughter from the audience. It would seem—though I am not going to attempt to judge motives here—that nothing less than a certain sense of solemnity would have accompanied confession of this sort. I could be wrong about this fact, however—and hope that I am. To make light of a 25 year or so charade as a "mid-life crisis" may have been due to *embarrassment*, but it seemed in bad taste.

At any rate, the case just mentioned is proof positive of the existence of detrimental teaching that has characterized a large part of the evangelical church. It is what Larry himself called "a trend that is moving the church toward irrelevance." Quite appropriately, he asked the pastors assembled at Moody, "What can I do that you cannot do?" The answer to that rhetorical question that he wished to hear is "nothing." About this, he is right on target. That question is a repetition of the so-called, simplistic nothing-buttery that we have been teaching for thirty years. So, Christian pastors, turn from the jargon of the psychologists to the truth of the Bible, and learn how to teach it. Others, while continuing to counsel informally, should leave the official work to the elders of the church who have been called by God and ordained by His church to that task.

There is more that could be said about counseling and the ill-effects that result from people taking upon themselves the mantle of "Christian counselor" without warrant from God, adequate knowledge of the Bible, and the requisite wisdom and prudence to do so. Let the warning have its intended effect. Surely you do not want to have to repudiate what you will teach and do for twenty-five years!

Chapter Four

The Relationship of Counseling to Teaching

If, as I have been saying, teaching is an essential element of biblical counseling, it will be of value to consider the relationship of each to the other. Teaching is but *one* necessary element in a process that also involves listening, encouraging, empathizing, admonishing and the like. In terms of the relationship of the two to one another, counseling, therefore, is *larger* than teaching.

That counseling is larger than teaching is an important fact. Because during the last thirty-odd years feeling, emotion and experience have been emphasized in counseling to the detriment of teaching and content, it is possible that in the next few years a reaction will take place. In any such reaction the tendency would be to swing to the opposite extreme, overemphasizing cognitive factors: teach people truth and they will respond positively. According to this erroneous notion, counseling virtually equals teaching. In an article in *The Christian Research Journal,* winter, 1995, Bob and Gretchen Passantino wrote, "This school, the cognitive, is one of the fastest growing schools in modern psychology (p. 23)." Nothing could be more tragic than for Christian counselors to swing to the opposite extreme in a reactionary fashion.

Certainly we must protest against both extreme views. The reaction that I have in mind may be creeping into the church already in some circles associated with biblical theology. According to some in those circles, contrary to biblical example and precepts, hortatory material ought not to be included in sermons. Moreover, Keswick-type teaching has for several generations stressed a quietistic approach to sanctification: learn the truth and yield to it. God will do the rest. At Keswick-sponsored meetings in Trinidad, when I was teaching Romans 12:13-21, some of the leaders expressed surprise at the fact that I encouraged action and obedience rather than simply calling for "yielding." The Keswick approach is very close to the other. Exhortations to *obey* seem all but nonexistent in these sorts of teaching; the Holy Spirit is thought to "do it *for* you *instead* of you." In any discussion of teaching in counseling, as a result, teaching must be given the place of an important, but not all-encompassing, element.

Just what does teaching do for counseling? What purpose and function does it serve in the process of changing believers so as to help them conform more closely to the Word of God? Teaching serves to accomplish two essential purposes:

  (1) it sets parameters for counseling, including goals and practices;

  (2) it provides the directions and information needed for counselees to know how to make changes that please God.

In short, teaching is associated with the acquisition of the fundamental materials for constructing a system of counseling and the biblical content from which the counsel that is disseminated to counselees is obtained.

Consider the former first. Many counselors think that they provide *biblical* counsel when they use the Scriptures in counseling. But we must ask, for what *purpose* are the Scriptures used? The answer to that question is basic to a determination of whether or not the counseling is truly biblical. The materials out of which a biblical system of counseling is constructed must be mined from the Scriptures and put together according to a biblical pattern. If they are not, the system—no matter how well-intentioned those who build it may be—will not be biblical. What do I mean by that? Simply this: you cannot construct a Christian system from pagan principles and practices.

Let's take an example. Many Christians today have become enamored with the Hallesby-La Haye Four-Temperament system. According to their belief, all persons fit one of four categories (or one of the blends of these). But where did this idea originate? It was the view of Hypocrites, a pagan Greek. According to him the four temperaments were the result of an excess or diminution of four humors (fluids) residing in the body. Temperaments, therefore, were determined by somatic factors. The entire structure of Hypocrites' theory collapsed when the four humor idea was proven false. To construct a supposedly "Christian" counseling system from materials salvaged from the ruins left behind after the demise of Hypocrites' humor hypothesis is to build using poor materials. There is nothing biblical about dividing mankind into four groups (or various combinations thereof) according to four supposed temperaments. Indeed, there is even less reason for Christians doing so than Hypocrites had!

Why, then, have so many Christians become enchanted with this defunct, unbiblical system? There are at least three reasons that can be given. First, the system is simple, easy to learn. It is even fun to place people in its various pigeon-holes. Secondly, the four temperament theory (despite protests to the contrary) lets people off the hook. You can hear its devotees excuse themselves for various behaviors with lines like these: "Well, you see, that's just how I am; after all, I'm a..." (and here they mention a supposed temperament type). Thirdly, they want to be biblical. Here is where many are attracted to this and many other false, basically pagan systems. In articulating the view, the fact that Hypocrites is its originator is either not mentioned or downplayed. Instead, much Scripture is used to support and illustrate the correctness of the view. Individuals from the Bible, like

David, Peter, John, etc., are said to fit into one of the four (or six-teen, if you prefer that version) temperament pigeon-holes con-structed out of the pagan materials. Whether they actually fit or not, each is stuffed into a compartment and thus *made* to fit. It is easy to do this by conveniently omitting certain traits or adding others that the text is *made* to teach about each. Thus the system is "validated" for the naive counselor because unless he thinks basically and digs deeply enough to examine the structure out of which the system is built, he may easily be taken in by the vast amount of the Bible used. But the supposedly strong point—the use of much Bible to support the view—is its weakness. How? The problem is precisely this—the Bible is *used*.

What do I mean by that? Just this: rather than going to the Scriptures to obtain principles and practices out of which to con-struct a counseling system, the four temperament counselor bor-rows a system already intact. He may modify it in certain respects, but the fact that it was hammered together by unbeliev-ers, from the world's materials (views), according to non-Chris-tian presuppositions, and provided with non-Christian principles, seems never to occur to him. The Bible is not used as the Source of the presuppositions and materials; rather, it is used to support the ideas embodied in the system. Indeed, to see this, and recognize the fact that there is no need to fit *biblical* person-alities into the pigeon-holes, is a dead give away. It might just as readily be your neighbors along the block. To use biblical per-sonalities to illustrate the principles, you see, does not make the system Christian; it only deceives many Christians about what is going on. In other words, biblical materials are used only to sup-posedly "validate" non-Christian concepts of God, man and the world. Because of this dangerous (near blasphemous) use of the Bible, people are duped into thinking the system is biblical. What they fail to see is that while much Scripture is quoted, this is done to support what is insupportable, namely, the adoption of unbiblical views that clash with the Bible. In the process, the

Bible is bent to conform to the system. *That is the wrong use of the Scriptures.*

Please don't get the idea that I am picking on the four temperament people. I have singled them out only because by analyzing a system so simple it is so much easier to demonstrate the widely-followed but faulty methodology used in constructing many systems of counseling that their devotees call biblical. In far more subtle ways, the same thing is done by others as well.

The other purpose of teaching in counseling has to do with the content learned by counselors and taught by them to counselees during sessions as the basis for analysis of their problems and the life changes that they must make. Because it is with this side of teaching that much of the rest of the book is concerned, I shall say little about it here. Teaching in biblical counseling leads to life-learning; it is teaching to *observe.*

Now, back to the *proper* way in which to construct a biblical counseling system. Let's consider a few examples, beginning with fundamental presuppositions. I shall mention only two (we *could* begin with the fall and subsequent nature of man, redemption and what it does, etc., etc.): the Bible is the inerrant Source of truth from God concerning life and godliness, and God provided in the Bible all that one needs for life and godliness. These presuppositions underlay all else. I shall not argue the first as it is an assumption held by all Bible-believing Christians. Those who do not accept this proposition could not be expected to concur with much else in this volume. If they have read this far, what I have to say probably is already being viewed with a morbid curiosity and superiority anyway! It is not for them, but for believers who are already committed to the inerrancy of the Scriptures, that I write.

It is, therefore, the second presupposition that is up for discussion among believers today. The subject is often referred to as the *sufficiency* of the Scriptures. The issue resolves itself into this: does the Bible supply *all* that is needed to develop a system of counseling and *all* that is needed to enable Christians to love God and their neighbors as God requires? Passages such as II Timothy 3:15-17 (especially v. 17) affirm the fact (see my book *How to Help People Change*, which is an exposition of these three vital verses) and the consequent "adequacy" of the "man of [from] God" who, using the Bible properly, is capable of bringing about the changes necessary for successful counseling. In addition to the passage in II Timothy, Peter says that God "has given us everything for life and godliness" through His valuable and great promises (II Peter 1:3,4). That is Peter's plain, unmistakable statement of the same truth that Paul penned in II Timothy 3. These verses record the fulfillment of Christ's prediction of the Spirit's work: "But when the Spirit of truth comes, He will guide you into all truth" (John 16:13). How? Consider John 14:26; 17:17.

These verses set forth clearly the sufficiency of Scripture "all truth" means all that is necessary for us to know (Deuteronomy 29:29). What a marvelous fact that is—the truly biblical counselor not only has truth, but *all* truth: all he needs to be thoroughly furnished for every good work, thereby making him adequate for the task of changing the lives of God's children in ways that will enable them to walk in God's paths of righteousness for His Name's sake.

Since, as we have seen, counseling is a matter of sanctification, making changes in lifestyle that are in accord with God's will, a matter of providing all that is necessary for life (eternal life = salvation) and godliness (behavior more and more pleasing to God = sanctification) is to provide all things necessary for *counseling*. If what He has provided in the Bible is sufficient for leading people to saving faith in Christ and for enabling them to grow in grace, then what He provided cannot help but be sufficient for Christian counseling. Notice how Paul's words have similar import: the Scriptures are able to make one "wise about salvation." They *teach* the way of salvation. But, being a God-breathed revelation, they also offer all that is necessary for "teaching" believers (they set forth God's standard for godliness); they "convict" (of sin when one fails to attain to that standard); they "correct" (point the way out of sin by repentance, confession and forgiveness) and disciple one by "training him in righteousness" (i.e., show him how to avoid falling into the same sin again in the future by replacing old patterns with new, holy ones). The process described in those words is a description of the process of biblical change that is brought about by ministering this all-sufficient Word in counseling. And if that were not enough, in three ways Paul declares the "man from God" (the minister of the Word) to be "adequate," through the use of the Bible, "fully supplied (or equipped) for the work of counseling, and for "every good work" to which He calls him in the process of changing the lives of the sheep in His flock. In the Scriptures, biblical counselors have all that they need to counsel. What more can they teach, what better can they teach than the all-sufficient Word of the living Creator?

So our proposition is that special revelation (the Scriptures) was given because general revelation (the knowledge of God obtained through the creation) does not afford knowledge of the way of salvation or sanctification. Special revelation was provided for the very purpose of doing what general revelation could not do. On this, note the division of the two revelations (and what each does) set forth in Psalm 19 (which, incidentally, is special revelation about both revelations—apart from which we couldn't even know those facts). Special revelation adds much more, but also interprets for us what general revelation is all about. Our understanding of general revelation would be impossible apart from Psalm 19, Romans 1, etc.

It is not right to speculate about what we may learn from general revelation concerning counseling as some have done. The Bible says nothing about learning anything concerning counseling from general revelation. Nor does it say that general revelation comes through unsaved persons (as is erroneously alleged by some who love to parrot, with little understanding, the sentence "all truth is God's truth." We can't even determine what truth is apart from special revelation). What it says about counsel from the lost is found in Psalm 1, where God warns against following the "counsel of the ungodly" and urges us instead to "meditate" in His Word "day and night." When we turn to the Scriptures, we find that to spoil the Egyptians of jewelry and of clothing is one thing, but to turn to them for ideas, beliefs, values, help that are the substance of the sort of thing one needs for giving counsel, he is forbidden to do so (cf. Leviticus 18:3,4; Jeremiah 42:13-22; 43:7). It is important not to turn to general revelation (or to unsaved persons, who have no revelatory powers at all) for the materials to construct a counseling system or for its content; these can be found only in special revelation. This is a fundamental presupposition.

So much for presuppositions (we could go on to list others, but this crucial one will have to suffice). What about *principles* that guide counselors? We said that these also are to be obtained from the Scriptures. Take a simple example. In Proverbs 18:13,15,17, for instance, utterly essential principles concerning listening (one element in counseling) are found. Nothing as simple, yet as trenchant, can be found anywhere else in the literature of counseling. The counselor who works out all of the implications of each of these principles of counseling and follows them will hardly go wrong. Their instruction is invaluable to him.

Another principle that guides biblical counselors is found in James 4:12. It teaches that no one is to talk about his brother negatively behind his back (the verb *katalaleo*, to "talk him down" is used). This principle governs all the Christian counselor does, encourages and allows in counseling sessions. He may not indulge in or permit others to talk negatively about persons who are not present. Remembering Proverbs 18:17, he encourages all involved persons to be present.

Another principle, rightly inferred from Titus 3:10, in contrast to those whose counseling is sloppy, disorganized and hit or miss, is that ordinarily sessions will continue over at least a period of a month or two. If counseling is to be cut short after one or two sessions, as Paul tells Titus, when it becomes evident that the counselee is schismatic, then one may rightly understand that he assumes sessions in larger numbers will often be held when the counselee shows no schismatic tendencies. Those who think that any contacts greater than one session long are unbiblical simply have not thought through the implications of this (and other) passages that indicate otherwise. I cannot cite all of the principles to be gleaned from the Bible for counseling in this place. Please see my many books on the subject for more. But these three are illustrative of what I am talking about.

Practices that are the natural and necessary outworking of biblical presuppositions and principles, as well as those specifically spelled out in the Scriptures, also must have their foundation in special revelation. These are numerous. The practice of church discipline set forth in my *Handbook of Church Discipline* is but a systematized statement of those teachings found in Matthew 18:15 and following, I Corinthians chapters 5 and 6, and II Thessalonians 3:14, 15. The very nature of teaching in the milieu (see Deuteronomy 6) and by example as well as by precept (see I Corinthians 11:1, etc.) are two practices crucial to all biblical counseling. The latter is not mere apprenticeship; as we study the gospel of John we see that it has theological roots in the interrelationships of the members of the Trinity itself. As we shall see, what to teach, how to teach it, etc., are all factors in one way or another taught in the Bible. These, of course, are but two examples of practices—that have to do with teaching in counseling—that are either biblically directed or biblically derived.

The ministry of counseling then, it is plain to see, is intimately bound up with teaching, which turns out to have an essential and central place in both the development of a biblical counseling system and the giving of counsel itself.

Just one other matter may be mentioned in closing. Biblical teaching enables Christian counselors to grow in wisdom and prudence, two characteristics vital to the pursuit of change in counselees. That one has the priceless privilege of working with the Word of the living God in counseling, with all of its attendant benefits, should not be down-played. It is a blessing no other sort of counselor can ever know in any other way.

Chapter Five

What is Biblical Teaching?

There might seem to be no need to ask the question: "Biblical teaching is the teaching of the Bible, isn't it?" Well, yes. Of course, that is true. But teaching the Bible can take various forms. And it may be done in a variety of ways. Some teaching may be made practical; other forms of teaching may not. Some teaching methods may be effective; others not. Some may be accurate; others far from it. And, just to develop the last issue a bit, teaching may be inaccurate in a number of ways.

When a passage of the Bible is taught, for instance, it may be taught for the purpose for which the Holy Spirit gave it. On the other hand, a counselor may ignore the Holy Spirit's purpose and use the passage for purposes of his own. While the former (*telic*) method of interpretation is always correct if properly done, the latter may constitute a serious misuse of the Scriptures.

Yet it is true that if the teacher-counselor understands the *telos* of the passage (i.e., the intention of the Holy Spirit in revealing it) and restricts himself to those parameters that are consistent with the *telos*, reasoning from it to some legitimately-inferred conclusion, the latter use of the passage also may be legitimate. But this indirect use of the *telos*, like the direct *telic* use, must always be done in harmony with and must grow out of the *telos*. So the matter, you can see, begins to take on a more intricate nature than might at first seem possible.

Apropos to the discussion of the nature of biblical teaching in counseling, in this chapter I intend to mention some necessary considerations by which you may determine whether any given teaching of the Scriptures in counseling is legitimate or not.

31

And, having determined that, I hope also to guide you into such usage in your own counseling.

To begin with, let's consider a scenario. A counselor is (rightly) concerned to help his counselee distinguish between outward conformity to a biblical commandment which he ought to obey and inner commitment. The problem upon which he is focusing is whether the counselee is doing what he is commanded *in order to please God* or not. Outward conformity fails to do this. The counselor speaks:

C: "So you see, Joe, it is one thing to do as God says in order to regain peace in your home [a goal that, in itself, is not wrong], but it is quite another to do it solely—or even primarily—for that reason."

J: "I'm not quite sure I follow you. Exactly what do you mean by that?"

C: "Well, as I said, fundamentally you must do what God says *in order to please Him*—whether that brings peace or not [here, the counselor quotes and explains Romans 12:18]."

J: "Hmmmmm..."

C: "It is all a matter of your heart. God sees not only your act, but the motive behind it. He says, 'As a man thinks in his heart, so is he.' Doubtless you've heard of that verse in Proverbs 23:7. In the light of the verse you must be sure your heart is right before God, not just right in your wife's eyes *in order to bring about peace*. After all, it is what you are 'in your heart' that counts. God looks at the heart; not only at your act. He cares deeply about your motives."

STOP! STOP! Think for a moment about what the counselor has done. First, he said many true things. His intention was biblically correct. He was definitely on the right track. But then he went astray. What is the *telos* of Proverbs 23:7? We are not concerned with the point that he is making; about that he is correct.

But we ought to be concerned about his use of the verse in Proverbs. From chapter 10 on, there are only a few places in Proverbs
where verses occur in a context. Most are given in isolation. It is
interesting, therefore, that this counselor (and we have read and
seen enough to know that the problem is widespread) has treated
the Proverb as if it too were given in isolation. It was not. What
is its context, and how should it influence the understanding,
meaning, purpose and use of the verse? In the section in which
the quoted material appears, the writer is warning the reader that
when invited to a dinner he ought to be slow about taking a second helping. The host may (insincerely) suggest that his guest
eat more: "Here, have another piece of steak," he may say, offer-
ing to pass the platter. "You'd better say, 'No thank you'," says
the writer of Proverbs. Why? Because the host really wants to
save it for tomorrow's lunch. What he's thinking *in his heart* is
not what he says with his lips. In other words, think twice before
taking another's words at face value under such circumstances.
What he says may be nothing more than a polite convention
(something like the southern, "Y'all come"). It you take him up
on his offer, he may say in his heart, "Why, that man's a hog!"
Read the whole section in a modern translation and see for yourself what the *telos* is. Clearly, viewing the proverb as a philo-
sophical or "psychological" understanding of man, given in the
form of a maxim, the way the counselor did, is failing to use the
passage for the purpose for which it was intended. It is an insight
for young men to help them to understand how to respond properly to ordinary conventions of the sort. Perhaps, then, you see
what I mean by the *telos* (or purpose) of the passage, and something of its importance. In this case, the counselor, with much
power and force, might have referred to Romans 6:17 where
God speaks through the apostle Paul of obeying "from the
heart." That verse clearly teaches the important truth that the
counselor wanted to stress. Indeed, because it does, the use of
Romans 6:17 in doing so has force and power that Proverbs 23:7

doesn't. All of which leads to the first element in any description of biblical teaching in counseling.

Biblical teaching is teaching that conforms to the Holy Spirit's intention. Every unit of material, no matter how large or small, if it is truly a unified section of the Bible, has a purpose. The primary task in exegetical and interpretive effort is to discover and fix that purpose (*telos*) clearly in your mind before using it in counseling. When you teach a counselee, therefore, you must be sure that you teach *telicly*. The counselor who misused Proverbs 23:7 failed to handle the passage accurately precisely because he misunderstood or ignored the *telos*. Any other use of the Scriptures in teaching will lack necessary authority and will misrepresent God. After all, to misuse a passage is to teach what God, the Holy Spirit, did not first teach. We are not only to think God's thoughts after Him (cf. Isaiah 55:8ff); we are also to teach His teaching after Him. You should not expect the Holy Spirit to bless your teaching when it is a perversion of what He caused to be written. None of us has the right to use passages for our own purposes. Of course, the Holy Spirit can bless the counselee in spite of a counselor's failure. But the counselor must be held responsible for his use of the Bible. For detailed information concerning *telic* interpretation, see my books *Preaching with Purpose* and *What to Do on Thursday*.

Biblical teaching is the ministry of the whole counsel of God. To *minister* the Word is more than merely quoting verses from the Bible. It is to properly locate, interpret, apply and implement those Scriptures, the *tele* (plural of *telos*) of which truly speak to the circumstances of the counselee. There are some who purport to do biblical counseling who reduce every problem to but one (e.g., "self" or "idolatry," etc.). As I noted, some quietists, therefore, understand counseling to consist of little more than getting counselees to "yield" to Christ (whatever that means). There are others who, having familiarized themselves with a half dozen verses or so, thus fortified, see all problems and their solutions (whether they pertain to drugs, marriage and communication breakdown, incest—or whatever) as coming under the aegis of these few verses. There may not only be laziness behind that sort of approach, but also a very poor understanding of the nature of the Bible. If they were correct, their Bibles would be only a chapter or two in length!

The fact is that Paul ministered "God's whole counsel" when teaching the Ephesians in counseling (see Acts 20:27,31). And in doing so, he spoke of not "holding back" anything that might be "beneficial" to them (Acts 20:20). Everything in the Bible has use in some situation. The problem with counselors who shrink Scripture to minimal dimensions is that they fail to acknowledge this fact. While there are certain verses to which one turns frequently in counseling (because they refer to commonly occurring problems or because of common misunderstanding of biblical teaching), he cannot afford to minimize others or shrink his counseling Bible to something like *The Reader's Digest Condensed Bible*—or less! God didn't waste space producing, or expect you to waste time reading, material that is of no use.

Biblical teaching is teaching that grows in fullness and depth. Of course, your knowledge of the Bible and how to use it in counseling will grow if you are faithful to the task. But that will happen only if you *never* become satisfied with what you know. No one in this life can ever attain an exhaustive knowledge of the Scriptures. One of the happy experiences in biblical counseling is the blessing of teaching a verse or two that you have just recently come to understand. You don't want to rush into the use of verses too soon, however, when you are not yet fully convinced of their interpretation. But to experience the joy of effectively using new verses in counseling, you must take the time for regular, in-depth study of the Bible, using commentaries and the many other helps that are available.

Biblical teaching in counseling involves explaining both the meaning of verses and a discussion of how they impact the

counselee. It is not enough, as some seem to think, merely to quote verses. The Spirit certainly may choose to use the uninterpreted Word, if He pleases (but don't forget Romans 10:14-17, which says He ordinarily uses the preaching and teaching ministry of the Word to do it). What the biblical teacher does is to so "open" (cf. Luke 24:27,32) the Scriptures that the counselee cannot help but see that the counselor is not advocating something of this own, but that it is *God* Who said what he is saying. That means that the counseling session, *in this way,* becomes (as it always should) a confrontation between the counselee and God Himself—not merely between the counselor and the counselee. *In this way,* the counseling becomes truly authoritative. No other counseling carries such weight. The commands, the warnings, the encouragements, the assurances, and the promises of the Scriptures introduced into counseling in this manner take on a quality that brings seriousness, hope and solemnity into the process. The power of the Holy Spirit, as He meets the counselee in His Word, is manifest in the effect that it has on those who realize the truth of what is taking place. In biblical counseling, then, the Holy Spirit is the principal Counselor.

Biblical teaching in counseling is clear, direct and to the point. Last week I received a letter from a correspondent in Finland who wrote,

> I wanted to write to you once again to express our gratitude for your short answer which was to the point, authoritative and convincing...I must add that, before we contacted you, we had asked for advice from Dr. Dobson's *Focus on the Family* staff, and their answer, though much longer than yours, was somewhat fuzzy, undecided, psychologizing, confusing. My sister-in-law was left hanging in mid-air, and she was so thrilled when she read your simple, biblical advice.... In your books, theology comes

alive, and the way you apply doctrine to real life is
simply unparalleled elsewhere today.

Now everyone who counsels, I suppose, receives letters of gratitude. It is not because of those words that I quote this letter. I
want you to notice the contrast that the writer sets up between
the vague, confusing response from the psychological camp and
the simple application of biblical truth to problems. One is
"undecided" and "fuzzy" while the other is "simple" and
"authoritative" (because biblical). While people tangle up their
lives in many ways—sin complicates—righteousness simplifies
life. The clear, straightforward approach to counseling from a
carefully-studied Bible is exactly what people in complicated
troubles need to free them from the entanglements of sin.

Complexity that results from the counselee's sinful living
patterns is best handled by calling first for repentance. Recently
two couples, up in years, came for counseling. One had gone to
several other "Christian counselors" with no results. The other, a
minister and his wife, had tried to solve problems according to
the advice that eclectic Christians had given in their books. To
no avail. In both cases, former emphases had been to go back
and rehash all the sins and problems of the past. This, naturally,
only made things worse. Instead of this, I called on all four to
repent, seek and grant forgiveness from one another, and thus
clear the rubble of the past so that we could build for the future. I
did emphasize that they could not just go through the motions;
the repentance had to be genuine. Otherwise they could expect
failure again. But I also explained that success in building the
marriages for the future was assured if they did as God wanted
them to do. I taught them the meaning and details about forgiveness, giving them a pamphlet I have prepared on the subject, to
help them recall the teaching they were given. They were told
what forgiveness obligates them to do. In both cases there was a
sense of relief and hope as, instead of dredging up the muck of
years, we put it where it belongs—in the past, buried, never to be

used against one another again. Of course, during these years
they had developed many patterns that were current. These had
to be dealt with in sessions to come, replacing the sinful patterns
that had caused so much trouble with righteous ones. The joy
that came to everyone when they kissed and settled down to
work on their futures is what few eclectic counselors see in an
initial session (if ever).

**Biblical teaching in counseling deals with sin, repentance,
forgiveness, sanctification and other theological matters.**
Man's problems are theological, not "psychological" (whatever
that means—few agree on a definition). If you want to contrast
biblical with eclectic counseling, turn to the indexes of the books
by those in the eclectic camp and you will notice an absence of
many such terms. While psychological jargon may abound,
theological terminology will be conspicuously missing. When
occasionally you discover a theological word (e.g. forgiveness),
be sure to turn to the passage(s) in which it is mentioned.
Chances are that you will be surprised (and saddened) to discover that it is misunderstood or misrepresented in a number of
ways. Forgiveness, used in the parenthetic example above, is a
typical example of faulty understanding. Recently even Dobson
has joined the crowd who speak of "forgiving God." He wrote
"...I am suggesting that some of us need to forgive God..."
(*When God Doesn't Make Sense*; Wheaton, Tyndale (1993), p.
238). This near-blasphemous (if not blasphemous) idea is widespread today. To take another example, if you read the term
"guilt," check it out carefully. Rather than reading of guilt as cul-
pability (as the Bible and good theologians understand it),
instead you are likely to read about subjective "guilt feelings."
Guilt before God is placed far in the background, if mentioned at
all. The stress is on alleviating the feelings. Also, the Freudian
concept of "false guilt" characteristically permeates books of
this sort. If you have any doubts about what biblical counselors
teach concerning these matters read your Bible. For a summary

of the biblical teaching on these matters, see L. Berkhof's *Systematic Theology*, my *From Forgiven to Forgiving* (on forgiveness) and, on guilt, my *Competent to Counsel* and *A Theology of Counseling*.

You would think, would you not, that Bible-believing Christians would see that the Bible's teaching regarding man's sin is a pivotal factor in counseling, since they know that it is the sin of Adam (and that of his descendants) that is behind every counseling problem one encounters. Think of it. Sickness and death, pain and suffering, envy and strife, murder and hatred, incest and adultery—you name it. It is all the result of sin. How utterly important it is, therefore, for every would-be biblical counselor to thoroughly understand the doctrines of sin and redemption. And he must know how to apply every aspect of these doctrines to the plights of counselees, whether it is their sin or the sin of others that has brought about that plight. Everything, from Genesis 3 to Job, from John 9 to Romans 5, Ephesians 4, and James 5, must be properly understood (if these references don't immediately bring teaching about sin to mind, you have study to do!). Biblical teaching in counseling is theological. That's the bottom line.

I could go on for pages describing teaching in biblical counseling. But this should be enough to convince you of the importance of it, and should give you a good grasp on the contrast between other systems and those that are truly biblical. Just as "all that glitters is not gold," so too all that claims to be is not biblical.

One final word. ***Biblical teaching in counseling promotes God's glory.*** That is not just talk. The Hebrew (Old Testament) word for glory is *kabod*, which means "weight." The Greek (New Testament) word for glory is *doxa*, which means "fame, reputation." In II Corinthians 4:17, Paul brings them both together to give the full picture of the meaning of the word when he speaks about the "weight of glory" *(doxa)*. When one truly glorifies God, he spreads His **fame** abroad by giving Him His full **weight** in whatever he does. I ask you, on that basis, which counseling system do you suppose glorifies God? One that touts the ideas and practices of men like Freud, Rogers, Maslow, and others who hated Him, or the system that brings counselees into confrontation with God and spreads His fame by giving Him and His Word preeminence in all it does?

Chapter Six

When Does The Counselor Teach?

One answer to that question is *always*. That is to say, in all that he does during counseling he is teaching. He cannot help it; by the nature of the counseling situation he will do so, consciously or unconsciously. Let's look at a couple of examples of this. If you are unaware of this aspect of teaching, it is time to alert you.

When, at your instruction, your secretary says to a potential counselee, "Your counselor would like to see both you and your husband," teaching (through her) has already begun. Negatively, you are teaching that you do not believe in and will not practice Freudian transference, in which the counselor and *one* counselee must meet *alone*. Positively, you are teaching that you believe the involved parties ought to be present. You are also teaching that you do not believe in negative talk about someone behind his back. You are implying that there will be a need for communication between the parties involved, etc.

When the counselor sits behind a table or desk (rather than in an easy chair), spreads out paper, his Bible, pamphlets, in front of him, taking notes and writing out homework assignments, he teaches thereby that he is interested in facts, not merely feelings, that he expects to get down to the business of *doing* something about the problem, etc. When he distributes booklets, pamphlets and other reading materials, along with weekly assignments, he indicates that he is interested in bringing about change and is working toward it. When he refuses to accept unfinished or unattempted homework, except for good and sufficient reasons, he shows that he is serious about this change. He is not there to waste anyone's time; he is ministering in God's Name. When the counselor "opens" the Scriptures, explains their meaning and helps counselees to see how the principles and practices taught or implied in them apply to his life, he is teaching that the Bible is practical and contains God's answers to human problems. In short, all that he does teaches.

That is why it is important for counselors to think deeply about and plan carefully all that they do in structuring counseling. The very structure of a series of counseling sessions, and each session in particular, should be considered not only with reference to its effectiveness but also in terms of what it *teaches*.

To sum up, everything in counseling should point to God and His power (not to the counselor). It should indicate that the Holy Spirit, working in His Word, is the One Who will bring about all the necessary changes in the counselee and his situation. All that contributes to that teaching should be included; anything that fails to do so should be altered or discontinued. The counselor has one teaching role: to communicate the counsel that God has graciously given in the Bible. So, counselor, you teach all the time. Never forget that fact. You teach the counselee something every time you do (or do not do) something in counseling. Both *what* you do and *how* you do it, therefore, are of importance.

But there is another way in which you teach in counseling. Whereas teaching by structure and practice that I have mentioned might be called *indirect* teaching (just to give it a name by which to identify it) there is also teaching that might be called *direct* teaching (again, a name I am using for convenience). Direct teaching takes place when both counselor and counselee discuss what Scripture says about how biblical passages relate to the counselee and his problems. It is this sort of teaching, no doubt, that you thought of when you responded to the question at the head of this chapter. Direct teaching, however, is not merely didactic; it too has its peripheral aspects, some of which are very important—indeed, at times these secondary aspects can become primary and may determine the outcome of the session.

I do not want to belabor the concept of *peripheral* aspects of direct teaching. But I should at least mention them and clarify what I am talking about. *Peripheral* aspects of direct teaching are to that teaching roughly equivalent to what connotation is to denotation in language usage. The choice of word can be all-important in conveying what one wants to say. Words carry emotional baggage as well as have sign value. When Paul used the word "Gentiles" (Acts 22:22,23) in the context in which he was speaking it caused a riot. It was like the spark that set off the explosion. So too, *peripheral* aspects of what one is saying can have strong import. Let's look at an example.

The counselor is not sure about whether or not it is possible for a homosexual to change. He has been swayed by liberal propaganda concerning the matter. So he fails to come out with a ringing statement on the matter such as, "God can forgive you and take away everything about this lifestyle if you mean business with Him. Let's look at I Corinthians 6:9-11 to see how He changed people in Corinth who were once involved in this sinful practice." Instead, he hedges, he "hopes" (the counselee senses, against hope), he "supposes." By all that he says and the words he chooses, though he limply says God may change the counselee, he conveys another message entirely. The counselee (consciously or unconsciously) gets the message (from the peripheral vibes he receives) that there may be some far distant possibility of change, but he should not expect it. The ringing affirmation, on the other hand, also conveys a message that supports and (indeed) enhances the words. One's attitude, enthusiasm (or lack of it) and his choice of words, along with the emphasis he puts on them, are some of the peripheral aspects of direct counseling that may be of supreme significance. If you cannot enthusiastically set forth a particular point of view with conviction and vigor, then don't attempt to counsel another about the matter until you can. Refer him to a biblical counselor who already can. And—this is of importance—study the question as the Bible speaks to it until you are firm in your belief.

Direct teaching is fundamentally of two sorts: general and specific. Certain biblical principles should guide all counseling. It is not necessary to review these teachings in each case if counseling is proceeding smoothly in line with them. Also, there are persons who, in your judgment, understand enough about them for you to assume that they will recognize that your counseling is based on these principles. On the other hand, sometimes, because of counselee violations, the counselor must take time out to present the biblical data, either because they are unknown by a particular counselee or because he has forgotten or purposely transgressed them. With reference to the last possibility, strong exhortations and warnings about the possible consequences of continued violations may be included in the teaching. When, however, violations occur "innocently" (out of ignorance or forgetfulness) usually nothing more than a didactic presentation (devoid of strong exhortation) may be necessary.

Let's take a look at an example or two. Bill and Mary have been having marital difficulties. Only Mary will come for counseling. As she enters the counseling room and sits down, her first words are "Let me give you something that I have been putting together for the last week."

C: "What is it?"

M: "It's a comprehensive list of all Bill has done to destroy our marriage over the last three weeks. Just read it and you will understand why I want to leave him!"

C: "Before we go any further, let me explain a few things, Mary. First, since Bill isn't here, and the Bible forbids both gossip and talking about another behind his back negatively [he explains James 4:12; see the earlier dis-

cussion of the passage in this book], I can't accept that
list at this time."

M: "But this is not gossip; it is truth—ALL OF IT."

C: "I am not accusing you of lying or even shading the truth.
But we must walk as far away from the possibility of
gossip as we can. Gossip isn't necessarily falsehood. It is
information that is shared with another to which he is not
entitled. It is information that it is neither necessary to
pass on (though true) or that God has declared it is
improper to share. In the present case, it is the latter that
is true."

M: "Well then, where does that leave us?"

C: "In a simplified position. You can begin by working on
your own sins and failures in the marriage. If you make
good progress on these, Bill may be more amenable to
coming with you to counseling—then, your list may be
of value. Even if we *did* consider Bill's faults today, it
would be worthless to do so; he's not here. We couldn't
talk to him about them. But you *are* here. And by God's
grace you can change. Let's begin by considering what
you do when you are frustrated, and any sinful reactions
you may show when you are irritated, etc., so that you
will be able to replace them with their biblical alterna-
tives."

The vignette you just read is an example of *ignorance*.
Mary's counselor had to correct her lack of knowledge by teaching her about essential biblical protocol that they must follow
during counseling sessions (which, it should be noted, are no
exception to biblical teaching about everyday behavior). Now
let's look at a different sort of teaching situation. This time it is a
matter of *forgetfulness*:

C: "Tom, Jane, if you don't learn to stop taking pot shots
and giving nasty, sarcastic retorts to one another like you

just did in that last exchange, I'm going to have to end this session right now!"

T: "Pastor, please don't. I'm sorry. I know it's wrong to speak that way to Jane, but it's a pattern I am trying to break. You know that I am. When emotion gets the better of me, I just forget and revert to my old ways. I'll try harder to remember—I promise!"

J: "Yeah! The same with me. I just find myself slipping into the old ways even though I don't want to. Forgive me, Pastor. Tom, will you?"

T,C:"Of course."

C: "O.K., I'm going to have to do something to help or we'll never get anywhere. In the future, I'm going to hold up my hand like this whenever it seems that you might be drifting into sarcasm and bitter words, to warn you to back off. Would that help?"

T,J:"Yes."

C: "Good, then let's begin where we left off."

Sometimes direct teaching has to be accompanied with help to enable counselees to put what they are learning into practice. It is important to reinforce teaching by reminders and by such helps.

Then there is a third way in which teaching is necessary in order to carry on effective counseling: you must learn to meet intentional attempts to stall, misdirect, circumvent or otherwise hinder progress. Listen to the following exchange:

C: "This is the second week in a row that you have not completed your homework assignment. Phil, is there some problem you haven't mentioned that is getting in the way? Until you accomplish this, we cannot proceed farther."

P: "Well, pastor, to tell you the truth, I just don't want to do it—you can understand that, can't you?"

C: "Sure. I can understand why you might not want to write that note telling your boyfriend that your relationship is finished. But you simply must do so. God requires it. Let me go over those passages we considered two weeks ago once again..."

P: "Pastor, that's not necessary. I know what the Bible says. I'm supposed to stop my homosexual behavior because it is an 'abomination' to God."

C: "Right! So let's write the letter. I'll help you if you don't know quite how to word it."

P: "No! I'm not going to do it. I just don't think it is fair."

C: "Well then, Phil, let me warn you about what God says must happen if you persist in your present determination to defy God."

P: "What's that?"

C: "I'll read you what Jesus says in Matthew 18 and in several other passages about church discipline. And I'll explain what they mean. First, note that He says,..."

The three scenarios above mainly have to do with teaching the counselee about how counseling must be conducted. That is the *first* sort of direct teaching that the counselor must be ready to give whenever necessary. Teaching of this sort may only touch the problem tangentially but yet it can be of major importance, as you can see. While it does not deal with the issue itself, what teaching about counseling protocol (biblical structure and process that is necessary for the proper conduct of counseling) does is make counseling possible. And it shows the counselee that in *this* counseling the Bible will be taken seriously. These rubrics may be peripheral but are important enough to teach.

Counselors may not relax any essential principles that govern and regulate counseling. Rather, they must teach and maintain them at all costs. But they may never *assume* that counselees know and understand them. Most do not. Many understand imperfectly. So from the outset, as well as throughout counseling sessions, there will occur times when it is necessary to stop and teach those principles. You can be sure, for instance, that most counselees do not understand the biblical stance on not granting *absolute* confidentiality ("I can keep this matter only as confidential as the Bible allows"), or your refusal to accept *privileged* information ("don't tell anyone I told you this, pastor, but you should know that..."), about *blameshifting* and many similar matters. At points where they bear on the progress of counseling, these things must be taught.

Don't look on time spent doing so as wasted time; it is not. In the long run (like Roberts' *Rules of Order*) this teaching facilitates what you are doing. It will keep you from many unnecessary tangles or complications as well as help you and your counselee to avoid a number of sinful pitfalls. Moreover, following biblical counseling protocol enables counselors to grow spiritually. These principles are, in fact, nothing more or less than principles of Christian living applied to counseling. They will enable counselors, as well as counselees, to grow by following God's Word more closely. Because the principles are Christian living principles, I have merely given examples of *what they are like* and *how they may be used* in facilitating counseling rather than attempt to compile an exhaustive list. As a matter of fact, in some way or other, probably every biblical principle could be of assistance in the work of counseling.

Now, turning to the sort of direct teaching that does involve issues confronted in counseling, we want to understand *when* such teaching ought to be given.

Often counselors must teach what God has said about issues raised in counseling. Not every counselee knows what God expects him to do. Sometimes counseling consists of little more than clarifying the exact nature and parameters of a problem, and then directing the counselee to the pertinent passage (or passages) in which a solution, or guidance in decision-making, may be found. Such counseling, though simple, may have profound effects. The entire course of a counselee's life may be altered significantly by the information you provide and the cogency with which you present it. You must be very careful to teach accurately and be sure to qualify your statements in ways that the Bible does. Much could be riding on your teaching.

Marvin came inquiring about how he ought to prepare himself for a future ministry of professional counseling. Should he attempt to obtain a master's degree or a doctor's degree in psychology from the university? That was his question. In response to some probing, I discovered that Marvin seemed to sincerely love people and wanted to help them. I inquired about how he thought he could help them preventively if he went into psychology. He had no answer to that; he had not thought along those lines. But he was intrigued with the thought; it was something that he agreed would be better than merely extricating people from difficulties. Yet he could think of no way to do this as a counselor. I suggested one. I explained that with his concern for people it was possible that God wanted him in the pastoral ministry, where every week, from the pulpit, he could do so. And he could do it in depth. I taught him from the Bible that counseling, as a life calling, belonged not to the so-called "professional" counselors but to *God's* professional, the pastor. He gave thought and prayer to this and now, as he told me when I recently met him again at a conference, he joyfully conducts a pastoral ministry of both preventive and remedial work, as all ministers of the Word properly do. The church, he came to see, is God's counseling center.

More complex teaching is needed in confronting issues. Divorce, remarriage after divorce, matters of church discipline, adoption, raising children, anorexia, depression all require teaching. One of the reasons for this is because there is so much widespread error about these and a hundred different matters. And, unfortunately, much of this error propagated by those who know nothing about the Scriptures has been brought into the church and propagated there as well. Much teaching, therefore, involves correction of false ideas. This should not surprise the Christian counselor; after all, much (most?) of the teaching of the New Testament is precisely of that nature. In a world of sin, in which the evil one has been tirelessly at work fomenting numerous errors on every front, that is what you should expect. After all, error can be multiple—there are any number of ways of going wrong (over 250 differing counseling systems in America today teach error about man and how to counsel him) but only one way to be right (God's way, set forth in His Word). It is very important then to learn how to challenge error, to refute it biblically, and to substitute God's truth in place of it. You can count on a majority of your counselees to have beliefs and convictions that must be challenged and corrected. You cannot avoid confronting error any more than the apostles did. It is endemic in sinful society and (if you read many of the books on the shelves of Christian bookstores) you will see that it is also rife in the church. *Confrontational teaching*, therefore, is another sort of teaching in counseling that you must expect to do.

It is important to confront counselees in the right way, in order to correct their faulty thinking. If you cannot defend your viewpoint by sane, reasonable, clear exposition of the Scriptures, perhaps you'd better wait until you can do so. If not, it would be better to refer a counselee to some pastor who can. But go along with him so you will learn how to do so in the future. It is not you who should confront the counselee, anyway. Remember what I said about the confrontation actually being between God and the counselee whenever you are able to show him what the Bible teaches. That is the proper thing to do. You are not interested in pitting your views over against another's; you want him to see that if he differs, it is with God Himself that he differs. You want him to be convinced by the Holy Spirit about the truth of the viewpoint you are presenting over against a wrong one. So, what is the way to do this? Like this: so plainly "open" the Scriptures that he cannot but help see (whether he initially admits it or not) that what he has thought is wrong and that what you are saying is right.

Not all teaching is confrontational but much, nevertheless, is *complex*. For instance, I have listed over a dozen questions that the Bible requires one who has obtained a divorce and wants to be remarried to answer the right way before the way is cleared. (I will not list them here since they can be found in my book *Marriage, Divorce and Remarriage in the Bible.*) If the counselor doesn't know about these, or neglects to probe according to them, his teaching may be inadequate or false—leading to all the bad consequences that may issue from it. To be certain that I don't omit any, I often turn to the list in the back of the book and make sure that I have covered all. Should I be embarrassed at possibly not remembering every item? Well, I ask you, should the pilot who consults his check list before taking off be embarrassed? Personally, I'm glad he does when I'm on the plane! It is important, then, to gain and remember details that ought to be taught in depth. Sin complicates (as I said before) and it often takes careful, complex teaching to extricate one from it.

Teaching in counseling also must be done from a broad knowledge of the Bible. While no one can be called upon to know everything in this life, the Christian counselor must have an ever-increasing understanding of Scripture that covers a wide variety of issues. He cannot keep but one page ahead of the counselee. He must be a teacher who is ready, prepared to teach upon every occasion on which the unexpected, unanticipated arises. That means he must ever increase his knowledge and understanding of God's Word. This, of course, is why James warns that "not many" ought to be full-time teachers. It is possible for the layman who counsels occasionally to say, "I really don't know the biblical teaching on this well enough, but I'll try to find out." Occasionally the counselor who counsels as God's professional may say the same—but *only occasionally.* If he does this very often, sooner or later people will begin to wonder why he doesn't know the answer. And they should; it is his business to know the Bible in a thorough manner.

When there is little time left in a counseling session and a matter arises that ought to be dealt with, what does the counselor do? Well, if time has run out and it is not possible to extend it long enough to teach the counselee something that he needs to know, a counselor may do one or more of the following things: (1) He can give him a book or pamphlet to take home that explains what he wants him to know. There are many of these, and every counselor ought to have a good supply of them. Perhaps he can hand him a "white paper" on the matter (i.e., a prewritten sheet on which he has detailed what he would have said if time had not run out); (2) He can schedule an emergency session in order to discuss the matter at the earliest possible time; (3) He can schedule a phone call with the counselee for later on in the day—or as soon after that as possible to complete the teaching that is necessary. Obviously many other ways to solve the problem could be devised, but these, perhaps, are the most common and most useful. The important thing here is to make the counselee aware that there is more to be learned than there was time to teach in the session because of time constraints (his or yours) and that he should not move ahead until information he lacks is imparted. Keep the counselee informed, at all times, about the state of affairs as you see it, so that he doesn't blunder ahead and create new and more serious problems.

Much more could be said, but let me close this chapter with a few don'ts: don't lecture your counselee about those things he knows perfectly well, don't go on and on wasting time repeating matters he already has grasped the first time through, don't stop teaching until you are sure that he understands (you can always ask him to put the teaching in his own words), don't teach him only a part (and not the whole) of what is necessary to accomplish the task before him (thus setting him up for failure), don't go into detail that is unnecessary to the accomplishment of the task and, when teaching, don't use too many don'ts!

Chapter Seven

Characteristics of a Competent Counselor-Teacher

In earlier chapters I have said something either directly or indirectly about this matter. For instance, I pointed out that the counselor should be "called" to the formal work of counseling by God and this call should be confirmed by His church; he should be knowledgeable of the Scriptures and he should ever increase this knowledge. Here I wish to elaborate on those themes from a different perspective and introduce a few new ones. I shall do so under the headings of *truth, life* and *ministry.*

TRUTH

If a counselor is to teach faithfully, he must know and love divine truth. There must be a burning desire, not only to counsel, but to learn all he can of God's truth. As a result, he will prepare for and develop skills in Bible interpretation and exegesis. If possible, he will acquire a working knowledge of the original languages, he will obtain and study as many of the existing study helps as he can, including the better commentaries, and he will spend hours devouring and mastering them. The time spent reading books about counseling (including mine) will be comparatively less.

He will soon develop a penchant for pouncing. "What on earth are you talking about?" you ask. Simply this: like a cat that sits waiting for a mouse, slowly swinging his tail—at ready to pounce on it when it appears—he too will develop a growing interest in pouncing on his own weaknesses and errors, anxious to correct and strengthen his knowledge and skills. Few things will make him happier than to discuss ways of becoming more biblical in his thinking and teaching.

As Jesus called Himself "the Truth" (John 14:6), so too does the counselor long to be known as a man of truth. He recognizes that what was perfect in Him can never be so in himself, so long as he lives this present life. Yet his great passion is to approximate as closely as possible the facts in the life of Christ that were the basis for this striking appellation that He applied to Himself.

A competent counselor-teacher knows his subject, but he also knows his counselee-pupils. The counselor, like His Lord, "knows what is in human beings" (John 2:25). He recognizes the far-reaching implications of biblical teaching regarding sin and redemption; he see that a knowledge of these is absolutely foundational to all proper counseling. He understands how only those who have been regenerated by the Holy Spirit can welcome, understand, appropriate and live according to God's truth (see comments in *The Christian Counselor's Commentary* on I Corinthians 2). He realizes that not all are equally educable. The unregenerate, on the one hand, must be evangelized before they become fit subjects for counseling; that is because counseling is a ministry that involves sanctification. Moreover, he knows that not every regenerate person is as educable as the next: unrepentant, and baby-like believers, for instance, must resolve certain problems with God and others before they can receive the truth they may need (cf. I Corinthians 3; Hebrews 5). He therefore has knowledge of the truth about man that guides and directs him in his dealings with counselees. He has learned that not everyone can be taught alike. It is not just a matter of native ability— which most everyone acknowledges—but also a matter of one's *spiritual* capabilities (as few seem to realize).

The competent counselor-teacher loves truth (not for its own sake, but because Christ is so intimately related to truth). Because of his love for truth, and for *the Truth*, he refuses to suppress truth (this is one of the sins of the gentiles mentioned in Romans 1:18). Nor will he shade or dilute it. He wants it to retain its sharp, pristine, biblical edge; in his teaching, he will not file that down. He will not stand with those who compromise truth in order to placate counselees. He will not allow error to prevail over truth; he understands that truth is from God. Nothing less honors Him.

The phrase, "the naked truth," has an interesting origin. It comes from a perceptive fable. Truth and error went swimming. Error emerged from the lake first and donned truth's clothing. When truth followed, he saw what had happened, but refused to put on error's clothes. Thus he was known as "the naked truth." How often error does parade around in the garments of truth! But, with truth, the competent biblical counselor-teacher will stand fully exposed for what he is and what he believes.

"Well, is it correct to say with many that 'all truth is God's truth'?" Of course, so long as you don't use that statement as a slogan to justify the incorporation of human error into your counseling system as many do. Since it is equally correct to say "all error is the devil's error," it is essential to know how to distinguish truth from error. The Bible alone is our absolute standard of truth. All other "truth" is likely to be partial or relative, and frequently suspect. It is only by using the biblical standard against which to measure any given "fact" or purported "truth" that one can be certain of its truthfulness: how little or how much it approximates the truth. Much of what eclectic counselors claim to be "God's truth" they simply *assert* to be such—with insufficient or no effort to discover whether or not it actually is. Biblical counselor-teachers always measure such assertions against biblical standards. The man of truth, who loves truth because it is associated with his Lord, is therefore supremely suspicious of everything outside the Bible that is called "God's truth." He wants to be given biblical proof for the claim; he will not settle for pious assertions. He refuses to relax his standards and declare something "true" unless he knows, for sure, that it accords in all respects with inerrant truth. *His* motto is John 17:17!

There is one matter that probably should be raised. There are too many persons going about declaring that all sorts of ideas they gleaned from unsaved persons are the product of "general revelation." That is in error. General and special revelation are *both* **revelation**. Revelation is knowledge given by God to man; not knowledge obtained by man using his natural capacities for subduing the earth. The creation does declare that there is a God and that He is a powerful Creator and a Judge. Psalm 19 and Romans 1 attest to that fact. That is general revelation. But I will not accept the idea that other redemptive facts given by God through revelation, or general knowledge derived from human effort to uncover information regarding the universe, is general *revelation*. Like special revelation, general revelation is *limited*. It covers only those things that the Bible says are appropriate to it. ***Revelation*** must be distinguished from all other sources of knowledge (whether it be general or special); it is inerrant. Ideas and facts obtained elsewhere do not share that characteristic. That puts them in quite a different realm.

Sometimes the words "general revelation" and the words "common grace" are interchanged. That too is a theological error. Common grace means the goodness of God in sending rain and sunshine, giving food and health to believers and unbelievers alike (Acts 14:16,17). It also refers to the restraints God places on human sin. However, since, by God's common grace, unbelievers have not lost all remnants of reason and logic nor ability to do science, it is possible for unbelievers to uncover facts (always misused and distorted because never related to God and His purposes) that make their lives and the lives of believers more comfortable. Indeed, it seems that because of their orientation to this world apart from God the ungodly line has been especially taken up with inventions, etc. (cf. Genesis 4:20-22). But—and this is crucial—it was not by general *revelation* that these things mentioned in Genesis were invented. It was merely through God-given human ability. Human discovery involves man taking the initiative, seeking facts; in common grace (as in all His gracious acts) God takes the initiative. Nowhere does the Scripture identify general revelation with common grace; that is a modern fallacy, which does little else but confuse an already complex matter. When you learn about general revelation in the Scriptures, it is limited to the knowledge of God. And common grace, which restrains evil men from becoming a bad as they might, and which allows them to do useful things in this world in spite of their sin, must *never* be confused with divine *revelation*. Unlike revelation, it is not a matter of inerrant, God-given truth.

LIFE

Truth is "in order to Godliness" (see Titus 1:1). The competent counselor-teacher sees Christ not only as the Truth, but also as the "Life." He is the One in Whom is life (John 1:4). He is the Source of eternal life and of abundant Christian living here on earth. He understands that it is truth that changes life and that life must be changed in accordance with that truth. Life for the counselor is the proximate goal for learning and teaching truth. Teaching involves teaching to *observe*. A biblical counselor wants to see counselees transform truth into life. He believes that one must learn (and he is supposed to teach them how) to "do the truth" (John's phrase) or "walk in the truth" (Paul's phrase). Truth, then, is a life-changing factor.

The competent counselor-teacher will neither learn nor teach truth academically, or abstractly. In harmony with his concern to learn the *telos* of each unit of biblical material that he studies, he will always learn and teach truth for its importance in life. He believes the Holy Spirit gave us truth in His holy Word, not merely to fill our heads with facts, but to achieve the life-altering *tele* (purposes) He had in view. To teach facts for facts' sake, or merely for the attainment of knowledge, *per se*, is therefore a perversion of truth. Truth is intended to lead to godly living.

The competent counselor-teacher will always be concerned to discover the purpose of each truth he learns and will endeavor to figure out how that purpose may be achieved in the life of each counselee. He is, therefore, an application-oriented student of truth. It is possible, of course, to understand a truth in a way that is unrelated to application in life. But, because of his *telic* focus on exegesis and interpretation, he believes that to do so is to fail to truly understand it. Until its application(s) to life is (are) known—at least to his own life—his quest for the full meaning of that truth is incomplete. It is, therefore, a practice of a competent counselor-teacher when studying Scripture to jot down life-applications of a truth that grow out of his understanding of the *telos* of a truth in its context. In short, his learning and teaching of truth is practical. It is life-learning and life-teaching in which he engages.

One other matter engages the minds of competent counselor-teachers in their study and teaching of truth: *implementation*. They know that it is possible for one to understand the meaning and intent of the Holy Spirit in inspiring a passage, but yet to have only the foggiest notion about how to transform that knowledge into godly living. They consider implementation of truth every bit as important as the application of it. In coming to this understanding, they recognize how Jesus spent much time dealing with implementation in the Sermon on the Mount. You read of Him saying such things as "When you pray...pray after this manner." The Lord's prayer, which follows, is a pattern given to enable Christians to know *how* to pray. It is implementation of the principles of brevity and non-repetition that He was inculcating; He was not framing a prayer to be repeated by rote. *How to* material in counseling, then, is a vital part of an effective counselor-teacher's repertoire. For more on this matter, see my books *Preaching with Purpose, Truth Applied* and *What to Do on Thursday.*

MINISTRY

Much counseling advocated in books today, like those Christians who read them, is self-oriented. What one can get out of counseling—that, and that alone—is the concern. Well, that is *not* the concern of the biblical counselor-teacher. In fact, for him that concern is only tertiary. First, all life-change must take place *in order to honor and glorify God.* I have already spoken about this in a previous chapter. One must want to change in ways that please Him, for His sake (Psalm 23:3). He must desire that change whether or not the change brings him those results he would like to have. Biblical counselor-teachers always teach that this, and this alone, is a sufficient goal because, as Jesus taught, it is the *telos* of the entire Bible to love God with all one's heart, soul, etc. Then he is to love his neighbor as himself as the second goal of life. His own welfare comes third.

Both of the love commandments (love for God and neighbor) pertain to *ministry.* The word "ministry" is simply another word for "service." We are to serve God and neighbor out of love. So a competent teacher will be concerned that the application and implementation of his counsel is not an end in itself, but is focused ultimately on serving God and neighbor. This means truth must be transformed into *life that ministers.* Every believer is to be first a servant of God, then of others. Paul loved to speak of himself as Christ's servant (slave). When you consider how fully the servant theme runs throughout the Bible, from Isaiah's Servant prophecies of Christ to the saints in glory ("His servants will serve Him;" Revelation 22:3; 8:15), you can understand the importance of this goal in life.

Since the sum of the commandments is to love God and neighbor, it is interesting to note that in the Bible love is often *commanded.* Love is not a feeling first. Rather, the essence of love is giving ("For God so loved the world that He *gave*; He loved me and *gave* Himself for me; Husbands love your wives as Christ loved the church and *gave* Himself for her; If your enemy hungers, *give...* "). Giving can be done in obedience to a command—whether or not you *feel* like it. Indeed, it can be done *against* all your feelings; it can be done simply to obey and please God. But when one gives enough, soon the feeling follows. The fact that loving is giving to God and to others, and the fact that ministry issues in service to God and to others, means that the two dovetail. The service that flows from godly living, which is the result of the assimilation of God's truth, is *loving* service. It is the result of love and, at once, also the impetus for greater love.

So these three remain: truth, life and ministry. But the greatest of these is love. Out of love born of truth, one *gives* himself to the assimilation and transformation of truth into life. And out of love that bursts forth from life, he *gives* himself to the service of God and man. All true teaching in counseling or elsewhere, for that matter, is driven by love. To put it simply, love characterizes all that a faithful counselor-teacher does.

It is important, then, to know that what characterizes the competent counselor-teacher is love. But that love is not amorphous; it involves intense study and accumulation of God's truth so that the counselor may have what is necessary to guide his counselees. It takes willingness to devote the long, tedious hours to the discovery of what that truth means in terms of holy living (both in the life of the counselor and then in that of the counselee). And it takes effort to work with the counselee to help him move from the self-focus with which he probably entered counseling (not *all*, but *most* do) to a ministry stance as the upshot of the change in his life that is effected by counseling. It is a glorious enterprise, counseling the saints—isn't it? Surely you who read about it must be challenged by what God's Word reveals!

Chapter Eight

Terms for
Teaching & Learning

It is instructive to learn from the vocabulary used something about how the Bible conceives of teaching and learning. While the study of terms in this chapter is not exhaustive, it will clearly acquaint you with biblical usage. Terms, unless fossilized in technical sediment, can be fluid, change with context and over the years come to have different meanings. They may also vary with context. Yet, if nothing more, they give at least a hint of what they originally meant when they were in pristine condition and less threadbare and worn. For that reason it is of value to examine both etymology and usage.

In the Old Testament there are four principal words for teaching, which are as follows:

1. *Lamadh*, which means "to beat" usually with a rod (or switch). This word appears in such places as Isaiah 2:3 where God is writing through Isaiah to rebellious children (see 1:2,3). See also Hosea 10:10,11. The word, as its origin and use suggests, stresses the need for discipline in teaching. The old ditty, "reading and 'riting and 'rithmetic, *taught to the tune of a hickory stick,*" says it all. The word, in its application to teaching, plainly acknowledges that many students, unless disciplined to do so, will fail to learn. Indeed, discipline, whether it be self-discipline (the ideal) or other-discipline, is essential for learning. This same thought is found in II Timothy 3:16 where Paul speaks of the Scriptures providing "dis-

61

ciplined training in righteousness" (see also Proverbs and
Ephesians 6:4).

2. *Yarah*, "to cast [or throw]" the finger out in order to point
the way. The idea behind this image is guidance, direction. In its noun form this word is translated "law," indi-
cating that the law points the direction for God's
people—the way in which He wants them to "walk."
Guidance is by the law. That it has not lost its original
import is clear from Genesis 46:28; Exodus 15:25, etc.
Teaching, according to this verb, is a matter of giving
guidance and direction to those who do not know which
way to go. It is a thoroughly anti-Rogerian word.

3. *Bin*, "to separate, distinguish between," emphasizes the
need for discriminating and discerning between things
that differ. An important element in all teaching is distin-
guishing the true from the false, the good from the bad,
the teaching of God from error, etc. One of the failures of
teaching in the modern church lies right here; many
teachers fail to make necessary distinctions. Thus doctrine is not sharply set forth and the minds of Christians
are muddled. See my book *A Call to Discernment* for a
full discussion of the biblical usage of this word. I shall
speak in a later chapter about the antithesis that the Bible
sets forth as an important aid to teaching.

4. *Ra'ah*, "to feed" a flock, speaks of the nourishing aspect
of teaching. People grow strong and healthy spiritually
when they are taught properly. It was Jesus Himself Who
stressed the fact that "man shall not live by bread alone
but by every word that proceeds from God's mouth"
(Matthew 4:4). The teacher must envision himself as a
shepherd of those he teaches, longing to see them thrive
on the good provisions that he feeds them.

In the New Testament, in addition to that which I mentioned above when citing II Timothy 3:16, you will find two principal terms for teaching:

1. *Didasko* is by far the most common word. It is a term that, like our word "teach" has no special emphasis. It is colorless, taking on whatever special meaning that the context in which it appears may supply.

2. *Paratithemi* means "to place beside," and has in it the idea of adaptation. It comes from the notion of placing something (in the case of teaching, data) at hand, where it can be easily acquired. It occurs in such passages as Matthew 13:24; Mark 8:6; Acts 16:34; I Corinthians 10:27; II Timothy 4:3 and Hebrews 5:12-14.

Every bit as instructive as these are the words for learning. In the Old Testament, the principal terms are:

1. *Sakhal means* "to become wise" by looking at or seeing. This describes the process by which one "sees" what he has not understood before. The idea closely corresponds to our expression when, upon comprehending something for the first time, we say, "Ah! Now I see." Obviously, like our term, it has its roots in ocular discovery. Yet, unlike ours, it probably retains more of the flavor of its root.

2. *Yadah* also has in it the idea of "seeing." The predominance of this way of speaking in Hebrew thought testifies to the fact that much learning was acquired, in large part, by teaching through showing. The word here comes to mean "to know" or "come to know" and, from the perspective of the teacher's activity, "to cause to know." Teaching was viewed not as a person spouting off material that was not comprehended by those who hear; it was considered to be a process that brings one to a state of knowledge that he did not possess before the teaching activity began. Learning was the process of coming to

know something with the help of one who *caused* the learner to know it.

The New Testament word is *manthano*, "to learn." The central thought in it, again, is that teaching is not the mere recital of facts before students, but the impartation of those facts in such a way that the students are "caused to learn them." Cf. Matthew 11:29; 28:19; Acts 14:21. Akin to this word is the frequently used term *matheteus*, "disciple, student, pupil."

While it is true, especially of the New Testament words, that the terms came to be used in a broader sense than they originally were, with connotations and even denotations that stemmed from the original sense, nevertheless it seems that the original thrusts of the words (especially those used in the Old Testament) were never totally lost. And in particular this is true of the subject in view—teaching and learning—since the concepts of teaching and the idea of learning were not only enshrined in the words used to depict them but also in the actual process of teaching which, in those times, did not change very radically through thousands of years.

As one examines these words, a couple of significant points emerge. For one thing, teaching should never be considered apart from learning. Several of the terms used have the two processes bound up together in them. A good teacher is one who elicits learning from his pupils. That means that he does more than deliver data. He delivers these data effectively. That is, he sees that the data are *learned* and *used for the purpose intended.* In this regard, he will remember Christ's words, "teaching them to *observe.*" (Matthew 28:20). Listening is not the same as learning. Again, teaching is conceived of not merely in didactic terms, but (rather) it is thought of as *show* and tell. Abstractions, we shall see, are rarely presented as such; principles are illustrated by narrative, parable, proverb, example, sign, token, etc. Teaching, in biblical thought, appeals as strongly to the eye and the imagination (the eye of the heart) as to the ear. Consider the following exhortations of Jesus, the Master Teacher: "Be careful about what you hear" (Mark 4:24); "Be careful how you hear [or listen]" (Luke 8:18). These powerful warnings about learning ought to speak volumes to both teacher and learner alike. When He spoke of the kingdom scribe (at that time a scribe was first and foremost a teacher), He pictured him as bringing forth "things new and old" (Matthew 13:52). That is another powerful statement to ponder. He teaches both fundamentals and that which is built on them. Again, with reference to His own teaching, He said, "everybody who has been thoroughly trained will be like his teacher" (Luke 6:40). It is interesting that in Mark 3:14 we read, "He appointed twelve that they might be with Him and that He might send them out to preach." In Acts 4:13 we read these telling words: "when they saw the boldness of Peter and John and realized that they were uneducated laymen, they were surprised and recognized that they had been *with* Jesus." Presumably Christ's teaching achieved its intended goal. How do we know that?

Mark tells us that Jesus chose the twelve to be "with Him." That is to say, He chose them to be His disciples. In His view of discipling, these twelve men were to accompany Him wherever He went, living, observing, listening, questioning, discussing. Note that Jesus did not ask them merely to listen to Him but to *be with* Him. That is a more comprehensive idea. It indicates an intensive exposure to Him—they heard, saw and learned from all He did and said over a period of three-and-one-half years. In Luke, Jesus' philosophy of education is recorded. In those words, "he will be like his teacher," He envisioned that larger purpose. To "*be* like" is much more than to "*think* like." Teaching today, if it is articulated clearly at all, comprises far less than both concepts. Indeed, the modern teacher often doesn't even require that his students *think* like him. (Usually he is happy if they think at all!) That, of course, is because there are few who believe that they have absolute truth to impart. But Jesus chose twelve to be *with* Him in order to become *like* Him and, to be sure, others recognized that they had been with Him because in some respects they had *become* like Him. That, in a nutshell, is Jesus' view of teaching. The terms "with Him" and "be like Him," therefore, are crucial phrases that describe biblical teaching.

Fearful as the fact may be for would-be teachers (remember James 3:1), teaching is the process of turning out others who, in thought and life, resemble their teacher. He, in turn, had better be a thorough disciple of Jesus—in all aspects. After intensive training of any length, others ought to be able to recognize the disciples of the one who trained them. What they say and do, and how they do so, are always apparent in pupils who have been effectively trained. Yet, at the same time, John, Peter, James, etc., were not carbon copies of Jesus or of one another; individual gifts and abilities were not destroyed, but rather enhanced, by their training under the Lord's tutelage. That means that being like Him meant like in essentials, unlike in individual ways that were nonessential elements in teaching.

The biblical word "wisdom" is another term of which every teacher ought to be aware. The word describes an entire genre of biblical writing, specifically, and the thought and understanding of an entire corpus of biblical writers. Wisdom is truth sagely and ably applied to living. The word carries connotations of knowledge used aptly and prudently. The wise man knows what to do, how to do it skillfully and in accordance with the will of God. He thinks and acts in the fear of God. Since the fear of the Lord is "the beginning of knowledge" (Proverbs 1:7) and "fools despise wisdom," no man can have true knowledge, or the wisdom that it begets, until he fears God. Teaching and learning, then, are done in the fear of God.

It is interesting to discover that the Bible is so deeply concerned with teaching (I have but skimmed the surface). As a matter of fact, teaching is a large part of what the existence of the Bible is all about. The favorite title by which Jesus was known is "Teacher." When He gave His church its marching orders, they were in educational terms (Matthew 28:20); and in one of His most tender and moving appeals He couched His words in similar language (Matthew 12:28-30). Words for teaching and learning like "take my yoke upon you" (mentioned in the previous citation) at first may not bring educational images to mind. But that expression was a Hebrew image for becoming a disciple. He "yoked" himself to his teacher. Frequently, in his writings, John Calvin rightly referred to the Church as "Christ's school." The justification of the believer takes place when he believes the "good news," the content of which, of course, he had to be taught. And half the task of the minister of the Word is to become a shepherd-*teacher* (Ephesians 4:12). All of this is important for the teaching that is done by counselors. To counsel effectively requires discipling, *causing* to know and helping counselees "see" all in a context of disciplined training in righteousness. In no other way can one be taught "to *observe*." Counselor-teacher, yours is no secondary task; it lies at the heart of our Christian faith.

Chapter Nine

Defining What You Have Considered

After several chapters of the discussion of teaching in its various aspects from a number of distinct perspectives, we are at last in a position to attempt a working definition of teaching in Christian counseling. That there is such a thing as distinctively *Christian* teaching in counseling I believe has been established to the satisfaction of any perceptive reader. I do not need to discuss that issue further. By distinctively Christian, I do not refer to the use of the voice, films, video, books, computers, turnover charts and chalkboards. There is, of course, nothing distinctively Christian about the use of these teaching tools. But if you are speaking about presuppositions, goals, resources, authority, content and basic methodology, the choices you make are decidedly Christian—or not. Computers and chalkboards are means; what one does with them (and how and why) has to do with methods. Methods employ means to attain the goals of a system of thought and practice and are inseparably connected to those ends. Methods = means committed to the ends of a system.

Here is my working definition of Christian teaching: ***Christian teaching is the vital communication of God's truth, in God's way, for God's purposes.***

Notice first of all that, according to this definition, Christian teaching is *God-centered.* The one teaching and those taught must take a back seat to the concern to please God. Any primary focus on man in an understanding of teaching (for instance, considering teaching *pupil*-centered), no matter how well-intentioned, misses the point. Ultimately that which makes teaching *Christian* is that at every stage in the process God is prominently in view. *A desire to please Him controls all.* God is not "brought into" the process; He is there—involved—in all that is done, from start to finish.

By *communication* I mean not merely the delivery of truth, but delivery done in such a fashion that the content of one's teaching is vitally received. By *vital* communication I mean that truth is actually assimilated into the thought and life of the one who receives it so as to effect those changes that God intended. Such assimilation, in contrast to mere learning *about*, constitutes what we may call *learning* in the biblical sense of the word. *Truth* is found in the Scriptures. This truth reflects the One Who is the Truth (John 14:6). All genuine truth is life-changing in a biblically-positive way and, therefore, useful. When truth is taught effectively (vitally) it always seems vital to receptive learners. They also know when it is not.

When I say that Christian teaching is a matter of communicating truth *in God's way*, I refer to the use of methods that are taught in Scripture by precept and example (e.g., Philippians 4:9) and those that grow out of and are consistent with biblical principles in every respect and at all points in the process of teaching. These methods are either directly given in, or are necessarily derived from, the Bible. They must never be imposed upon it from the outside.

The phrase, *God's purpose*, has to do with both the biblically expressed objective of glorifying God by wholeheartedly loving Him and one's neighbor and those proximate goals that lead to this end. To glorify God in teaching is to represent Him properly in relationship to all that is said and done in teaching, thus according Him His due weight so as to increase His fame in the eyes of counselees. God is glorified when counselees are brought face to face with Him in His Word.

Having said these things, let us apply our working definition
to the slice of an actual counseling case in order to see how it
impacts teaching in counseling. A husband and wife go to their
pastor for counseling. They are members of his church. He is
contemplating a divorce; she does not want one. He has come for
counseling only with the greatest reluctance. He may even think
that if he can prove that there is no hope for their marriage, he
may be able to justify a divorce. The conversation begins as follows:

H: (disgusted) "I really don't care to be here; I've come only
to get her off my back. She's nothing but an insufferable
nag!"

W: (infuriated) "Well, of all things! That's a rotten accusa-
tion. And what do you mean by it? I thought you said
you wanted to save our marriage, and that you'd come to
get help."

C: (relaxed, but firm) "Perhaps we would get farther, with
less strain, if you addressed your remarks to me rather
than to one another. It seems apparent that (in addition to
whatever other problems you may have) you don't know
how to talk to one another helpfully in order to deal con-
structively with problems in the way that God requires in
Ephesians 4:29 [which he reads and explains]. No wonder you are having marital difficulties that you cannot
solve. As we go along, in addition to whatever else we
do, I'll try to teach you some of the important principles
of communication that the Bible sets forth. Without
them, we can do little about other matters. But first, we
have to look into an even more basic matter—your reasons and expectations in coming for counseling.

How does our definition fit what is happening thus far? The
husband has said that he doesn't want to be there. He has come,
he declares, to get his wife off his back. That is an inadequate
reason for a Christian to seek counsel. His agenda must be chal-

lenged and altered before fruitful counseling may begin. The
counselor is aware of this; that is why he is about to consider
"reasons and expectations." Nagging, communication, etc., are
put on reserve for later; they cannot be avoided, but are hardly
matters with which to begin. Nevertheless, a modicum of proper
communication is necessary to proceed. That is why he must get
control of the session and guide it into the proper channels. Otherwise, if he allows nasty words, accusations and rejoinders to
prevail, counseling will go nowhere. That is why he gives some
minimal instruction concerning how to talk *in counseling*. And,
what is of great importance, he indicates thereby that God cares
not only about the marriage, but also about how they address one
another in discussing their problems. God, and His controlling
Word, are apparent from the outset. Biblical truth has been used
helpfully. We continue:

W: "Well, I guess that's true if anything is, pastor. We certainly *don't* know how to communicate."

H: "We haven't talked about anything important for years!
   Why bother to communicate? All I ever hear from her is
   'buy this' and 'buy that,' until I'm sick and tired of being
   used as nothing more than a money supply source!"

W: "Hrmmmmph! *You* should talk! You could supply more
   if you'd stop loafing and get up off your duff and sell
   more cars. We hardly have enough money to pay for the
   kids' tuition at college, pastor."

C: "Please, Nancy, try not to address Tom directly at this
   point. You two have to learn how to talk in ways that
   please God. As I said, we need to examine why you are
   here and what your expectations are before getting into
   issues like money, laziness, nagging and so on. Tom, is it
   true that you came here (as you put it) simply to get
   Nancy off your back? Wasn't there any other expectation
   you had beyond that?"

H: "Well, that was a good part of it!"

C: "Was the other part of it a slight hope that you might be able to rebuild your marriage in ways that please God?"

H: "Of course I'd like to, but there isn't much hope that it will happen. You can see what we're like. You can see what I'm up against. What can you do with a woman who has only one interest in life—money?"

C: "What I'm interested in, Tom, is whether or not you are willing to make a serious effort to rebuild your marriage according to the blueprint found in Ephesians 5 where God describes marriage in terms of the relationship of Christ to His church."

H: "I certainly can't see us ever coming even near that. We're so far from it we can't even see it, let alone reach it."

C: "You may think so now, but if you mean business with God you can progress in that direction a lot faster than you may think. Tell me, Tom, do you believe that God is able to transform your marriage into something good and pleasing to Him?"

H: "Well...I guess He is *able* to; but He sure isn't doing it. And I don't see any hope of that in the future."

C: "That's probably true as things stand, but if (as I said) you mean business with God, and commit yourself to obeying His Word *in order to please Him*, you can expect His blessing upon your efforts."

H: "I suppose you expect us to pray about the marriage. Well, let me tell you—prayer hasn't accomplished anything so far."

C: "No. I don't expect you to pray. And it would be wrong for me to advise it; you are in no condition to pray."

W: "What's that? What do you mean?"

H: "Yeah, you'd better explain that; I don't get it."

C: "It's very simple. Let me read I Peter 3:7 for you [he reads]. You see, Peter is saying (among other things) that when you learn how to treat your wife properly, and start treating and talking to her as a Christian should, then—and then alone—God will listen to you. But until then, God says, 'Don't talk to Me, because I won't pay attention to your requests. Your prayers have been "interrupted" by your sin.'"

H: "Well, that's a new thought to me. I was sure you'd tell us to 'pray about it' the way most Christians do."

C: "Prayer is important, in the right place and under the right conditions, but in your present condition, with you dickering about rebuilding your marriage or not, God won't hear you. You are a double-minded man. According to James, you shouldn't expect anything from the Lord. We've got to get you to the place where He will hear and answer again."

H: "That sounds like a different approach. I've wondered for a long time why my prayers were not being answered. Do you think that will really work?"

C: "Of course it will. When God promises something, He keeps His promise. You see, God is not a cosmic vending machine that delivers cans of coke when you deposit the correct prayer coin. He's a Person. And that means that He bears a relationship to you. When that relationship goes sour, you shouldn't expect anything from Him. You must sweeten it again through repentance."

H: "I see."

C: "Now, let me ask you this: do you want to restore proper relations with God by rebuilding your marriage or not? You know what is right before Him. But there must be a commitment to do so before we can go ahead with counseling."

What has been going on? Fundamentally, the following:

1. The counselor has worked toward and has succeeded in gaining control of the session, even though it began haphazardly (as many do).

2. He has avoided discussing issues between Nancy and Tom, important as these may be, and has moved counseling toward a more basic matter: commitment to rebuild the marriage *in order to* please God, thus restoring the broken relationship with Him and regaining access to Him through prayer. At this point, Tom is clearly a double-minded man who, until he settles this matter, as James says, "shouldn't suppose that he will receive anything from the Lord" (James 1:7). He knows God's will about the matter, but he isn't sure he wants to make the effort to do it. In that condition, counseling cannot progress farther. That is why it is so important to get the matter settled right away. His sin against Nancy (and who knows who else) and His hesitancy to acquiesce in the will of God have built a barrier that must first be overcome. It is clear that Nancy's bitter speech grieves the Holy Spirit (cf. Ephesians 4:29,30) and must be dealt with in time. She also may have an idolatrous attitude toward what money can buy. In time, the counselor will have to investigate thoroughly Tom's charge about that matter. But not yet.

3. Initially the counselor has focused his attention upon Tom. Why? Not only because he is the one who is so tentative about counseling and who might otherwise not show up again, but because he is the head of the home. As such, he bears the principal responsibility for doing something about it when things go wrong. The counselor is moving in that direction and will soon make that point.

4. The counselor deflected the concern from difficulties between Nancy and Tom to the more critical problem of

difficulties between them and God. God has been accorded His proper weight in the matter. It has become clear that He is the primary One with Whom these counselees will have to do, as the counseling proceeds. This is utterly important.

5. The counselor wants commitment to God's will in order to please Him as the primary objective (not to gain peace in the marriage). The decision Tom must make is not whether he wants to rebuild his marriage but whether he wants to please God. That is where the counselor (rightly) has steered the discussion.

6. The pastor has brought Tom face to face with God in all of this, as he ought. The question no longer is whether or not Tom wants counsel but whether he will commit himself to pleasing God. His final answer will be given to God, not merely to the counselor. The matter will be worked out more fully as they proceed, but so far, counseling seems to be moving in the right direction.

7. Teaching has been taking place all along. Indeed, it is the "new" teaching about which Tom remarked that seems to have snagged him in spite of himself. He expected to hear that trite, old advice that gets nowhere in these sorts of situations, "Just pray about it." Instead he was told—what he knew already—that it wouldn't work. Instead he learned something new as the counselor taught him, using the Scriptures *telically*, why it wouldn't work. Tom seems to be getting hope precisely because of this new approach stemming from a "new" insight into biblical teaching. Bible truth at last is becoming vital. Teaching that focuses directly on what God has said about the problem seems to be precisely what intrigues him. It has given him new hope. Automatically? No. But through proper explanation and application as his counselor teaches him. The counselor trusts the Spirit of God,

dwelling within Tom, to use His Word when interpreted and applied rightly, to speak to him about his condition.

I could enlarge on this counseling case, showing where to go from here, but from what you have seen so far it should be plain that, from start to finish, behind what is done are the views that have been set forth in the definition above. That definition, and my discussion of it, should provide a sufficient sample of the important place that a sharp understanding of teaching plays in counseling. Unless you know what you intend to do, it is certain that you will not be able to reach correct goals. That is why it is of value to summarize your thoughts about teaching in counseling in a succinct, yet comprehensive form. Perhaps when you teach, my definition (or your modification of it) will help keep you on track. Would you like to place it under the glass on your desk for reference? Unless you have something of the sort to go by, what will you use as a guide?

Chapter Ten

Fundamental
Laws of Learning

It is important to understand something of the laws of learning as they are set forth by Jesus and others in the Bible. The Bible is a book about learning. It is a teaching volume. Consequently Christian counseling—which, as we have been saying, includes teaching—is committed to helping counselees learn. If we understand these laws, then we can conform our teaching to them. If one fails to teach in the way in which students learn (or ought to learn) his teaching may turn out to be something less than teaching in the true biblical sense of "causing to know." In part, or whole, it may be little more than beating the air with words.

In this chapter, let me quote two verses from the words of Jesus from which we will take our start (there will be more about learning in subsequent chapters). He said, "Be careful about what you hear" (Mark 4:24). In Luke, we read the companion statement, "Be careful how you listen [hear]" (Luke 8:18). In both references Jesus plainly warns that it is possible to hear (or listen—the original terms are the same: the verb is *akouo*) carelessly. Careless listening is what He describes in His parable of the sower. Seed is sown by the good Teacher, but teaching (effectively causing to know) is hindered by soil which is not receptive. Various causes of this non-receptivity are listed. It is these that we now want to examine.

To begin, we must say a word or two about the word translated "be careful." In both passages the word is *blepo,* to "see,

perceive, discern, consider, take heed." The word is properly
translated "be careful" or "take care," as comprehending the full
thrust of the word that may be seen in the terms used above to
translate it. It is about as comprehensive as our word "see." The
idea is to have enough concern to do whatever is necessary to *see
to it* that one hears the right thing ("what") in the right way
("how"). Those are the two emphases of the Lord in the passages
referred to. Interestingly enough, the verb also occurs in Luke
8:10 where Jesus says, quoting Isaiah 6:10, "though they *see*,
they won't *see*, and though they hear, they won't understand"
(*suniemi*, "to bring together, to perceive, understand"). Jesus is
deeply concerned about the care one must take in order to
"understand" (which here He indicates by quoting the Isaianic
parallelism of three careless ways of understanding, i.e., to *see*
and to *hear* with comprehension). Understanding with comprehension, according to the Greek verb, comes as one compares
one statement of fact with another, after weighing each individu-
ally, and then placing them together in a meaningful way. The
characteristic of a good hearer, therefore, is his ability to assimilate and make sense of various truths. So the Lord wants no
sloppy listening. He calls for effort, thought and reasoning about
the teaching of the Word as it applies to himself. *What* one is to
hear is God's Word; *how* is to hear it with understanding that
leads to obedience.

In the parable of the sower (we will use Luke's account in
chapter 8 as our basic source), Jesus is setting forth laws of
learning. The good seed is sown (in this case by Him), but there
are various responses to it—according to the conditions of the
soils upon which it falls. The seed, He says, "is God's Word" (v.
11). There are three initial sorts of responses (described under
the figure of the seed sown and the results obtained). The first
group "hear" (v. 12), but the devil soon comes like a bird and
"takes the Word from their hearts." They are not saved because
they were like hard ground into which the seed never penetrated.

As it lies there on the road surface, the birds come and eat it. In other words, Jesus says, to receive the Word, one must not be hardened against it. The devil has no difficulty in distracting any such person from the message; it never gets into him at all. These are people who resist the truth (they don't like it; they want nothing of it, so they harden themselves against it).

The second soil superficially covered rock which lay just beneath. People of this sort are emotionally attracted to truth (they "hear and receive the Word *with joy*") and seem to "believe," but there is no moisture (regeneration); the seed, though going down into soil, fails to take root. These are superficial persons. What they hear sounds good, and thereby gives them joy for a time, but when they learn what Christianity is all about their so-called faith dries up. Emotional attachments remain only until emotions change. They are unstable; their "faith" does not endure.

The third group is that large number of persons who hear, but decide against the faith because other things (like thorns and weeds that choke it) are more important to them. These are those who make the wrong choices in the light of the options. They are too engrossed in the things of the world—"worries and riches and pleasures of life"—to allow Christ to take first place in their lives; indeed, to do so might mean the loss of some of these things: some of them don't hear as they ought because of fear.

But notice, in each case they "hear" (cf. vv. 12-14). Yet in each case also it is said that they hear, "but." They lack an open, wholehearted desire to learn the truth. No wonder Jesus' comment in verse 18 is "Be careful *how* you hear." The way in which each of these heard was faulty—and led to eternal condemnation. How should one hear? In a helpful summary regarding the good soil that "produced fruit a hundred times over" (v. 8) Jesus' comment is, "And those on the good soil are those who, when they hear the Word, hold on to it with a fine and good heart and persevere until they produce fruit." The difference is in the heart attitude. The ability to apprehend, hold on, and persevere is precisely what the former three responses lacked. And the reason was the condition of the heart. The heart of man is "deceitful and desperately wicked" (Jeremiah 17:9), and needs to be replaced with a "fine and good" one since it is a "heart of stone" that is resistant to the things of God (Ezekiel 36:26). The fine and good heart can only become a reality by regeneration of the Holy Spirit (see also I Corinthians 2:9). In other words, the Word of God must be received in genuine faith that will persevere. Whoever perseveres to the end will be saved.

In the Mark passage, it is the *content* to which one listens that is stressed: "Be careful about *what* you hear (Mark 4:24)." The world around, that tells us to get all we can while we can since we only go round once, convinces those who seem otherwise interested in the gospel that it is not worthwhile. After all, they have no root; so "when affliction or persecution comes about because of the word, they stumble right away." Their interest is "short-lived." They want things here and now; they don't want to suffer pain or loss. The laws of learning, as Jesus set them forth, are these: Learning takes place when one is serious and diligent enough to "take care" about what he listens to and how he listens. He cannot be concerned about other things to the extent that he makes wrong choices, that he cares only for the immediate pleasure that he might receive or that he will not persevere through affliction should it come. Obviously faith involves a steadfast trust that will "hold on" to the truth and not let go under pressure. Truth (and *the* Truth) must mean more than anything else or any one else, including one's self. Jesus' basic call, then, is found in the words of Mark 7:14, "Listen to Me, every one of you, and understand" (cf. Matthew 15:10). But to understand, one must listen with a fine and good heart.

It is commitment to *truth* (about which I have already said a good bit earlier) that is basic to the understanding of what a fine and good heart is. Note, conversely, that the heart that makes no such commitment is wicked. Jesus makes it very plain that the reason people don't hear as they should is because, as He put it, they are from their "father the devil" (John 8:43,44). One must belong to Jesus Christ and have God as his Father to understand truth (cf. I Corinthians 2:14). Jesus had to "open" hearts in order to enable people to hear and believe (Luke 24:25,45).

To take care, as that exhortation applies to a believer, is not much different since the very same things tempt the believer that tempt the lost—even though he knows better and is basically committed to truth. He is not yet perfect. The worries and cares of this world, pleasure and the fear of persecution are likewise problems with which he must deal.

Let's think of those for a minute. Notice, they are not *intellectual* problems. To fail to hear correctly, to misunderstand truth when it is presented, is fundamentally a *moral* issue—as, indeed, all these matters that Jesus mentioned clearly are. When worry overcomes faith in a loving, caring heavenly Father (Matthew 6)—that is a moral problem. When one wants to be accepted by the world, so he fudges on his beliefs, trims his sails on what he teaches or how he counsels—that also is a moral issue. Whenever a believer refuses to do the hard work of exegesis, but settles for emotionally-pumped up froth instead, there may be instantaneous "joy," but it won't last. Nor will it satisfy the Lord's command to take care (see to it) that he hears well. That also is a moral problem. So what I am saying is simply this. It is fundamentally a *moral* problem that confronts us when we don't understand Christ's clear, simple, loving truth.

Let's pursue that fact further. What sort of things get in the way of hearing? Well, we mentioned resistance. Whether it be prejudice ("I'm a Methodist [or whatever] and I'll always be a Methodist") or whether it is a matter of faulty presuppositions ("the Bible is only one source of truth for life and godliness"), the matter is the same. To the extent that the heart is not as fine or good as it ought to be, it can be closed to truth. Counselors will find teaching difficult for this reason. They will have to appeal to their counselees to be *willing* to learn, not to resist as unbelievers do. Often when counselees act like unbelievers in face of the truth of God, it is not a mere difference of opinion that is at the bottom, but it is a moral problem. When believers won't listen *carefully* (won't look to the way in which they listen), it may be because they have sloppy study habits, because they have never taken the time to learn how to study the Scriptures, because they hear only partially (or selectively) or because they want to learn without effort. Those too are moral issues. If teachers take the time to prepare and present truth carefully, it is incumbent on those who listen to exercise the same care in hearing. Then there are those who hear only so much because they recognize to go further in their understanding might mean they must discontinue certain shady practices, change their style of living, become more ethical in their dealings with others, or something of the sort. For instance, Christian counselors cannot ethically take Medicaid or medical insurance money when they (avowedly) claim not to be doing medical work. There is no way to fudge on this matter and still be in accord with Christian truth. So some would rather not hear all of it; they draw the line on how much truth they receive because they want to continue to draw the line on this lucrative source of income! That is a moral problem. One could go on and on with such illustrations, but those mentioned sufficiently paint the picture of why many do not hear, even though they are Christians—or Christian counselors! Watch out for those who alter, filter, shape or selectively use the truth.

Of course, the pride of life as well as the cares of the world get involved. These matters are not always easily separated. Someone has taken a stand for some error (he once believed to be truth)—perhaps he lectured or even wrote books that taught it. Now he realizes that he was wrong. How easy it is to stand by that error rather than to submit to truth. Pride may be so strong that he will convince himself that his error is God's truth. There are hundreds of ways in which counselees will refuse to change their thinking because of pride. You will soon run into the full complement if you do any counseling to speak of!

And finally it would be wrong not to mention those who "hear" God's Word but fail to "do" it (or do very much of it). They don't learn because they don't do. Their attitude reflects something of the attitude of the man who built his house on the sand (Matthew 7:24,26). In other words, that which keeps people from immediately grasping the truth in a firm grip as they hear it proclaimed is—pure and simple—*sin*. The sin may be of one sort or another, it may be a matter of mixed motives, but whatever its form or complexion, it is sin! To learn is to learn to *observe* (Matthew 28:20).

Consequently there will be times when, in order to help counselees, these matters must be addressed. The counselor-teacher will discover that teaching is not a matter of delivering truth to the pristine minds (blank slates) of counselees who cannot wait to hear and do the truth. Rather, in order to teach, at times he will discover that he must first call them to repentance. He must bring them to see the sin that stands in the way and to deal with it. Otherwise it may be impossible to progress farther in counseling.

The fact that because of their failure to grow, many counselees are like babes that cannot learn the weightier matters of Christianity but must be fed with milk, is also noted in Hebrews 5 and I Corinthians 3. They are not yet able to understand more because they have been so lethargic in their Christian lives. Indeed, as Jesus said, "Whoever doesn't have will have even that which he seems to have taken away from him" (Luke 8:18; see also Hebrews 5:11 to see how Christians can grow "dull of hearing"). For more on this matter, see my detailed discussion of it in *A Call to Discernment*. But once again the writer to Hebrews and the apostle Paul treat the problem as a moral one. That is the

principal fact. The laws of learning boil down to this: One learns
when his heart is fine and good (a moral issue), so that he is open
to God's truth more than to anything else in the world and will
persevere in it no matter what may come his way. That is what
Jesus was teaching us in his important discussion of learning.
Learning theories have little or nothing to say about the moral
matter. No wonder there are so many of them; people are still
searching for the core issue. At the heart of the issue is something more basic than all else—how dearly does one love truth
(and *the* Truth)? That is the question and that is the matter that
the counselor-teacher must keep in mind at all times as he han-
dles a counselee's failure to understand.

To say that teaching must accord with Christ's laws for learning is to say that one ought to present the truth in a manner that
exalts it above all else except the One Who is the Truth. Of
course, to exalt it as His truth is the same thing. He must be hon-
ored throughout. Moreover, the counselor-teacher must help
counselees to understand that what they are dealing with is precious, something that must be handled with extreme care and
must be obeyed at all costs (cf. Matthew 28:20). The world
knows nothing of Christian truth. It is devoid of the understanding of the purpose and meaning of life and the world. How marvelous it is to know these things. When the counselor makes it
clear that he respects the truth with which he is dealing, something of this will rub off on counselees. The care with which he
attempts to understand and teach it, the concern with which he
calls for conformity to it, the caution with which he presents it—
his general attitude toward the Word—all these contribute to
successful teaching. Teachers sloppy in their handling of the
"word of truth" (II Timothy 2:15) only contribute to the failures
of counselees whose basic faults in understanding are moral. His
teaching, to put it briefly, therefore must be every bit as moral in
all respects.

Chapter Eleven

Reaching in Teaching

As I have noted, the biblical concept of teaching includes learning; unless someone has learned, teaching has not yet occurred. That is a far distant cry from the sort of teaching that some of us received. I can remember a teacher at Johns Hopkins University saying, "It's not my job to do anything more than give you data; I don't care if you learn them or not. That's entirely up to you." Now certainly there is responsibility on the part of the learner (as I have also noted) but that does not preclude the task of the teacher to *make learning possible.* The Christian teacher's responsibility, then, extends beyond the mere presentation of facts.

Teaching, in accordance with this idea, involves **reaching** the student. That means he may not present truth in such a manner that it is difficult to understand or obscure. Rather, it is his job to so teach God's truth that—so far as he is concerned—there is nothing more that he can do to "get it across" to his pupils. If they fail to appropriate it, that must be entirely their doing. He will have fulfilled his part. So, while the student may not necessarily give assent to what he teaches and may fail to apply it to his life for his own benefit, that failure will not be because he does not know what to do or how to do it, or because he was not encouraged to do so. That is what this chapter is all about.

The one who *teaches* in a manner that *reaches* is one whose teaching **reaches the heart.** But, like the difference in the soils upon which he sows his seed, the results may be good or bad, good or better. The teacher's task is to sow—faithfully—so that

85

he penetrates all obstacles to learning. He must reach the heart of those to whom he speaks. The two results, elicited from two sorts of hearts (those that are regenerate and those that are not), are clearly exemplified by the two responses found in Acts 2 and Acts 7. In the first instance, Peter's teaching fell like good seed on fertile soil, soil that was plowed and disked by the Holy Spirit in response to Christ's prayer from the cross (Acts 2:37; Luke 23:34). In the second instance, it fell on stony, resistant soil (Acts 7:54). Yet in each case we see that the message got through; it *reached* those who heard. While the Christian counselor is working with believers, who possess all the resources to understand and assimilate truth, they are not always ready to do so; like unbelievers, they may be very resistant. Irrespective of receptivity or of resistance, the true teacher makes certain that his message gets through, that it reaches the heart.

Sometimes people speak of the "unction" of the preacher or teacher (some popular preachers have spread about this unbiblical idea) as opposed to the lack of it as the reason why the message does/does not elicit a positive response from the listener. But the fact of the matter, as we clearly see in the two instances cited, is that *both* were filled with the Holy Spirit. So, while the teacher is responsible to teach the Scriptures in such a way that the message gets through, he is not responsible for its effects. The differences in Acts 2 and 7 were not chargeable to the condition of the speaker (Luke indicates that both were Spirit-motivated) but to the heart conditions of the hearers. In both chapters, Spirit-filled teachers penetrated to the hearts of their hearers; in one case there was receptivity leading to repentance; in the other fury leading to murder.

What is this "heart" that must be reached (penetrated by "piercing" [chapter 2] or "sawing through" [chapter 7]) by the teacher? It is the *inner person*. Unlike Western teaching, in which emotion or feeling is equated with "heart," in the Scriptures "heart" refers to the inner life of the person that he lives before God and himself. This life is fully known to God alone, partially known to the person himself and unknown to others. Often it is the inner *as over against* the outer person (in contrast to the lips, the mouth, the hands, etc.). Heart, in the Bible, never is opposed to head (or intellect) since it includes the inner reasoning and thinking processes (Hebrews 4:12, for instance, speaks of the "thoughts and intents of the heart"). To reach the heart with the Word of God, which is "sharper than any two-edged sword," is the task of the teacher ministering the Word in the power of the Holy Spirit. To reach the heart, then, is to genuinely reach the listener. It is to reach his motivational center. That is teaching in the biblical sense of the term. It is the communication of God's truth in such a way as to be understood correctly and to elicit a response that indicates the fact—whatever that response may be.

As Hebrews 4 indicates, the Bible is designed to penetrate to the heart. But failure to use the Bible properly (because of fear, human traditions, etc.) can make the Scriptures "of none effect."

How then does one "reach" the hearts of those he teaches when counseling? The principles are the same as those involved in doing so when preaching (after all, preaching and teaching in counseling are but two sides of the same ministry of the same Word). The rest of this book will be dedicated to the discussion of the various principles and practices that may be followed, along with a survey of many techniques that may be employed in doing so. But before turning to such matters I shall devote the remainder of this chapter to a discussion of two factors basic to all the rest. They are **clarity** and **boldness**.

I shall consider it conceded that Paul was a master teacher. Yet, great teacher that he was, he thought boldness and clarity so important that he asked the churches to pray that he might not be deficient in these two areas. He seems to have singled them out as two imperatives of Christian teaching and preaching (in both key places where he asks for prayer that he may be bold or clear

he appends the comments: "as I ought to" and "as I should"—
Colossians 4:3,4; Ephesians 6:20). That the apostle was so concerned about these issues should cause us to be concerned as
well.

Let us first consider *clarity*. Nothing is more essential. How
dare those who teach what they purport to be God's Word be
fuzzy or obscure? This is not a message from a friend, from an
employer, etc.; we are talking about *God's* truth. We dare not do
anything to distort that truth either by taking away, adding to,
weakening or altering it.

While I make no judgment as to his motives, it is curious that
Tillich, who in his sermons made his message utterly transpar-
ent, showing that he was fully capable of doing so, for some reason or other, wrote in the most crabbed, obtuse fashion when
composing his two volume theology. Some, because they think it
will impress others, like to become obscure. Others want to hide
the reality behind jargon. Still others are muddled-thinkers who,
if they were more lucid, would be judged as such. And still others are simply poor writers. While none of us is perfect and we
all have a long way to go, it should be our intention not only to
learn and know the truth of God as fully as possible, but also to
proclaim it from the pulpit and in counseling as clearly as we
can. That means thought, work and practice. It is not enough to
obtain truth. It is also essential to consider the best way to communicate it with the least amount of loss or addition in the most
comprehensive way we can. It means taking care about *how* we
teach. It means considering the state and knowledge of those to
whom we speak, etc. All too few counselors care enough to take
the time to improve their teaching skills. The main aim in doing
so is not to be able to call attention to how well one speaks, but
to eliminate everything that confuses or obscures. The goal is
clarity. In improving, then, the counselor must think about what
it is that makes his teaching less than lucid. Many of the principles and practices of teaching that will be set forth in succeeding

chapters are designed to help do just that—teach clearly by *eliminating* whatever obscures.

The second element is **boldness**. There is no more pervasive theme throughout the book of Acts than the boldness of the apostles. In Acts 4:13, for example, we are told that it was the boldness of Peter and John that revealed the fact that they had been with Jesus. Boldness—the ability to speak truth without fear of consequences—was, indeed, what they prayed for (Acts 4:29). And it is what the Holy Spirit provided (Acts 4:31). In this chapter you have the Christian teacher's prayer. It makes it clear that in order to "speak" God's "Word" one *needs* boldness (Acts 4:29). No wonder that Paul and these apostles prayed for it. Boldness is absolutely necessary to proper teaching. For whatever reason, it is possible to dull the truth of the living God (why one would desire to do so is almost inconceivable).

Do you pray for boldness and clarity in your teaching; do you ask your constituency to do so? Others must be taught the absolute necessity of these two factors in all true teaching. Where they are not present truth may not reach the listener's heart. The filling of the Spirit brings about clarity and boldness. The two items are related. If one is bold but obscure, the boldness will not of itself cause the truth to penetrate; it will probably only annoy. If, on the other hand, one is clear but not bold, clarity will not make up for the failure to teach all that one should out of fear of reprisal.

So, as we proceed, let us keep in mind that all we learn in subsequent chapters will be slanted toward bringing about clarity and boldness, on the one hand by the elimination of obscurity and on the other by the elimination of fear. The key word here is *elimination.* When these things are eliminated, the Holy Spirit fills the void!

Chapter Twelve

Preparing To Teach

As I have previously pointed out there is a wider scope of teaching for which one is responsible when he seeks to counsel than when he preaches. In preaching, the teacher prepares beforehand the materials to be understood and communicated on a given day, knowing that these are what will be the concern during the sermon. No matter how fully one attempts to prepare beforehand for a counseling session, however, there is no guarantee (apart from an inflexible, frozen, ineffective approach) that he will even be able to *open* the session with a discussion of the matter that he prepared to teach, let alone continue to focus on it throughout.

Why is that? Because the ongoing circumstances of counselees change from session to session. You may be thoroughly prepared to teach your counselees how to communicate, at the outset of the session in which you plan to do so, when the husband announces, "We have decided since we saw you last time to get a divorce." Obviously the thorough preparation for this session that you made must be set aside and an entirely different matter must be considered. In seeking forgiveness from his boss in accordance with a homework assignment, a counselee instead may have further agitated him by attempting to justify his reprehensible conduct contrary to the advice you gave him. As a result, he has lost his job. That changes everything. Since the previous session, a member of the counselee's household has been take ill. Priorities have changed; the time that would have been used to work on certain problems must now be postponed because of the necessity of daily hospital visits. Teaching further truth under these conditions would be fruitless. And so it goes.

Because life is so unpredictable, it is impossible to plan with certainty what one will do or teach at any given session. The counselor's knowledge of the Scriptures and how to apply them must be widespread, and his ability to act flexibly and teach whatever is necessary about the circumstances at hand is essential. As I have already noted, until (and unless) one is able to attain to this place, he ought to proceed very slowly with counseling. That statement is not intended to scare off those who ought to be doing counseling as a life calling. Rather, it is intended to urge them to get whatever help they need. It is important not to go off half-cocked into the field of counseling not knowing what is involved. Just this week I spoke to a woman who said she was doing counseling and wanted to develop a counseling center. In our discussion it turned out that she didn't even know what counseling is. What she was calling counseling was actually evangelism. While in most cases that sort of basic ignorance will not be the case, yet all sorts of people, it seems, for a wide variety of reasons, want to become involved in counseling. In many (perhaps most) instances they are sorely unprepared to do so. How well prepared are you?

What, then, does it take to prepare for that for which you cannot prepare? It takes a *general* preparation that extends over the entire corpus of Bible doctrine and knowledge. That means a grasp of systematic theology. It means an ability to be able to locate pertinent passages having to do with the whole counsel of God. It means an understanding of the plights into which sin has plunged people. It means the ability to apply and implement biblical truth to many situations. How does one obtain such information? In other words, who will teach him to teach?

There are, of course, a number of ways in which such preparation may be obtained. A good seminary education is at the top of the list. There are also many books and tapes now available (write to Harrison Bridge Rd. Bookstore, 257 Harrison Bridge Rd., Simpsonville, S.C. 29681 or call [801] 967-2986 for a list of these). Courses are taught at annual and regional conferences of The National Association of Nouthetic Counselors, 5526 SR 26 East, Lafayette, Indiana 47905 and year-round by The Christian Counseling and Educational Foundation, Chestnut Hill, Pennsylvania, 19118, as well as in many other places. *The Christian Counselor's New Testament* is a new translation that includes helps for counselors covering the major issues they may encounter and highlighting passages that may be of use in dealing with them. It is a work designed to be used in counseling to facilitate the use of the New Testament. The book *What to Do on Thursday* was written to give knowledge of how to turn from a problem to the Bible in order to find and use the Scriptures in helping counselees and others. Used in concert with others as a course, or alone in one's own study, this book will provide what many need to gain a wider knowledge of the Bible for use in counseling. Two other books, *The Christian Counselor's Manual* and *A Theology of Counseling*, also will be found helpful. There is, then, no reason why one who lacks what is necessary to do effective counseling may not prepare himself for it.

Preparation, in this general sense, is absolutely necessary—and it will be ongoing. No one is ever able to say (accurately) that he needs no more preparation. But, as he studies issues with enthusiasm and dedication, he will discover that he is developing a new confidence that will go a long way in counseling. Yet, if he begins to become overconfident, he may expect the Lord to throw him a curve that will strike him out, bring him to repentance and send him back to the Bible to study it with new vigor. Counseling regularly raises either new problems or old ones in new configurations. That is why one must learn flexibility and ever continue to prepare.

The only other way to prepare is not to prepare. That is, one may learn in the arduous, destructive manner of "learning the hard way," i.e., by trial and error. The trail of ruined lives that one who does this leaves behind him is more than enough reason to abandon any such thought. Of course, it is not possible to learn everything before one begins to counsel; otherwise, he would never counsel. That means *unintentionally* he too will learn some things the hard way. But he may never adopt that approach as his basic method of learning. God is gracious to give you cases you can handle as you faithfully study His Word in order to prepare for them. A biblical counselor, therefore, does not follow Dewey's principle of learning by doing; rather, he learns *for* doing. Dewey had no standard or source of truth; the biblical counselor does. In learning *for* doing, the biblical counselor sets his goals (we have discussed these) and then he learns what it is necessary to know by way of information, skills, etc., in order to achieve those goals.

When you do not know what to say in a particular counseling session, don't bluff your way through. Admit the fact. That will not lessen the counselee's trust in you—indeed, it should enhance it. He sees that you refuse to bluff or speculate. Then, during the following week, find the answer either by studying the issue further or (if that fails) by consulting others who do have the answer (e.g., people on the NANC list—obtainable from NANC headquarters in Lafayette). But if change is the order of the day in counseling, and a counselor cannot depend on meeting conditions that are consistent with those he encountered at the previous session, can (or should) any preparation at all be made for an upcoming session? Yes. One ought to prepare as if the next logical step were going to take place, as if he were not going to meet change. That has definite advantages. First, it enables the counselor to deal with those times when change in conditions does not occur. Though I have emphasized the need for flexibility to meet changing conditions thus far, let me hasten to say that there certainly are times when counseling proceeds exactly as it ought. In such circumstances, you will know what to do because you were prepared. Secondly, you do not waste the work that you do in preparation, even if at the next session you can not draw on it. Later, after other intervening matters have been cleared up, you will be able to fall back on that preparation. And even if you never get to use it in a given case—for whatever reasons that preclude it—you will have widened your response repertoire and you will be able to use it in the future in some other case. Moreover, often *portions* of one's preparation may be used in the upcoming session. Sometimes the change in circumstances is not so radical that everything must go. And even when you must forego using the whole in this session, if you have a pretty good idea of where you wanted to go and how to get there you can often sketch that for the counselee in order to bring hope.

"What do you mean?" you ask. Well, suppose some matter has intervened to impede progress and must be dealt with before you can proceed further. At some point you might want to say to your counselee something like the following: "I had hoped to go on to teach you how to solve the problem with your son today. In doing so, I had intended to discuss such and such and so and so. But we must postpone that discussion till we clear this new matter away." If what you were going to do is something that the counselee wants very much to learn, to tell him this should be an incentive for him to work hard on the immediate problem that interrupted. If you hadn't planned a course of action, you could not sketch its outlines for the counselee. As it is, though truncated, you can still use that preparation in the current session in this way.

Preparation involves not only what to say, but also how best to say it. An approach to one counselee may not be effective with another. You must take into consideration the knowledge that each counselee has. In one case, the explanation of what you are teaching must be more comprehensive than in another where there is already a basic knowledge of what is required. Moreover, the attitude of the counselee is important to consider. Is he willing to learn or not? And, of course, the basic ability of the counselee to understand and appropriate teaching is important. A child may or may not be able to comprehend what an adult can. In still other instances the prejudice, false ideas, shoddy doctrine of the counselee may get in the way and, therefore, must be eliminated. I cannot raise all of the possibilities here— nor would you want me to. But from these few examples you can see how important flexibility is. It is not only important in moving from one matter to another depending on the changing circumstances in the life of the counselee, but also in presenting the same material to a different counselee.

A study of the sermons and the speeches in the Book of Acts will demonstrate how the same teaching had to be adapted to different audiences. There were Jews and Greeks, country bumpkins at Lystra and sophisticated philosophers in the audience at Athens. There were illegally acting members of the Sanhedrin in one gathering and a courtly retinue in another, etc. In each case, the apostles adapted (not the teaching but) their presentations of the gospel. Counselors must learn from this. They must learn to prepare and use examples appropriate to children and those that are appropriate to adults, those that fit educated counselees and those that best convey truth to the uneducated. They must learn when to go into detail and when to simply sketch what is necessary to know and do, according to the alacrity and attitudes of particular counselees. In other words, flexibility in counseling requires flexibility in preparation. Some counselors are able to adapt on the spot; others (probably most) are not. That means counselors must think out the various possibilities beforehand. Naturally this cannot be done so that there are no surprises, but those who have done much thinking and preparation beforehand will encounter less.

There is another sort of preparation that, once you use it, you will say is necessary. I refer to the purchase of giveaway books and pamphlets, and the use of prewritten materials of your own. In this day of personal computers and desktop publishing and laser printing it is possible to prepare attractive materials of your own. Prepared materials demonstrate the right sort of professionalism, that problems are not unique and that there are known solutions to them.

The chapters that follow are designed both to show you the sorts of things that you must learn in order to prepare for counseling and to provide examples of actual materials that may be used. I hope you will find them helpful.

Chapter Thirteen

Teaching and Language

True teachers of every sort recognize the importance of the language they use in teaching. It is their stock in trade. Not only must the counselor's speech be clear and bold (see Chapter 11), it also must be accurate and appropriate. It is difficult to overstate this point in the matter of counseling. People often enter counseling sessions emotionally charged, confused or filled with fear. Under those conditions, one must be sure that what he says is apprehended correctly by the counselee. Often this requires utter simplicity of statement, repetition and the like. Indeed, it is wise to write out main points and weekly assignments and even, at times, to ask the counselee to explain these in his own words.

Moreover, the field is replete with jargon. I recently corresponded with someone who considered my concern for accurate language pedantic—or at best fastidious. He thought it satisfactory for a biblical counselor to use psychological jargon to attempt to express biblical truth. That is an error of judgment that can have serious consequences—the words you use carry freight; that is why the Christian should avoid all such jargon and use only those terms that truly convey what he wants to say. He was trying to teach responsibility while using the language of irresponsibility. The problem was not with my correspondent's view of counseling but entirely with his view of language. I have noticed that the problem is widespread—even among those who, otherwise, are genuine nouthetic counselors.

I said that language carries freight. It is the vehicle for transmitting thoughts and concepts. That God endowed man with language and has deigned to speak to him in language should make us highly appreciative of the process He chose to communicate truth. Because it carries freight, it must be examined to see what sort of denotations *and connotations* certain language usages have in certain contexts. Words may not be used carelessly (or even casually). One must think through his use of terminology. Otherwise he may convey meanings he never intended, thus leading counselees astray and defeating his own ends. There is enough confusion in the mind of the average counselee; the counselor does not need to add to that confusion by poor use of language!

To call someone "schizophrenic," for instance, is to say little or nothing. I am not referring to Karl Menninger's delightful comment about the word ("To me it's just a nice Greek word") but to the facts that 1) there is no longer a universally-accepted definition of the term, 2) its original meaning has largely been abandoned and 3) the word denotes an effect (that may have widely varying causes) and not a disease or single etiology. The word schizophrenia simply tells us that someone has been behaving in a manner that is socially unacceptable. It is, therefore, pure jargon; it signifies nothing useful. The same is true of much of the language employed by psychological counselors: it confuses, covers ignorance, mystifies laymen, etc., but fails to enlighten. Though the terminology sounds impressive, when examined it proves to be as vaporous as a soap bubble. How much better it would be for the Christian counselor-teacher to say that a certain counselee has been behaving in a way that is unacceptable, and it is necessary through counseling to discover, if possible, what it is that is causing the abnormal or bizarre behavior. It could be sleep loss, drugs, a brain tumor, etc. But to use one technical term to describe behavior that stems from widely-differing causes like these is unhelpful. It covers up the real facts, makes counseling harder and confuses those who are involved. Often, as Crabb observed, such terminology even can become a cover for one who is *pretending*. True Christian counselors must never confuse or pretend.

Of greatest import is the fact that when you search the Bible for a solution to a counselee's problem you do not find terms like "schizophrenia" or, let us say, "dysfunctional behavior." Again, this latter term says nothing about etiology; it describes only what physicians would call "signs and symptoms" (but not of one, clear-cut disorder). The counselor who digs deeply enough into the causes of so-called "dysfunctional behavior" will discover one sinful pattern or another at work. Why, then, not say that "sinful persons are behaving sinfully" and begin to sort out and work on the sinful patterns? Such terminology may not sound as impressive, but it is certainly more accurate and helpful because it reveals the cause of the disruption and, by implication, points to the solution in Christ. Now we can apply a scriptural analysis to the problem and discover a biblical solution to it.

Biblical counselors—so far as possible—ought to use terminology given by God (cf. I Corinthians 2:13, CCNT). Use of biblical terminology leads to the discovery of biblical solutions. The biblical counselor-teacher should teach biblical truth in biblical terms so far as is possible. In *The Christian Counselor's Wordbook,* a small volume I wrote some years ago (that I hope shortly to bring back into print), I listed, defined and discussed a number of terms that Christian counselors will find helpful to use in describing the problems that they encounter in counseling. Moreover, in the back of *The Christian Counselor's New Testament* (TIMELESS TEXTS, 1995) there is a list of critical issues to each of which is attached key Bible verses that deal with it. That is something with which you definitely ought to familiarize yourself.

In teaching counselees your speech ought to be vibrant, colorful, hopeful and (at times) even shocking—never dour or stuffy. It ought to convey assurance, confidence and authority that are demonstrably based on God's promises in the Scriptures, not on one's own ability. In dealing with sin the counselor should not express horror or shock, but (while never condoning sin) his language should always point to the forgiving wonder of the cross. There is where one finds the solution to the problem of sin. He should speak of confession and forgiveness; and he should use simple, biblical words in doing so. He should abandon academic language; in this he should take his cue from the Bible Itself—preeminently from the language of Jesus. In the choice between dry, dull speech and that which is at once colorful and memorable, there is no question that he should opt for the latter so long as it is precise and accurate.

Counselors also would be wise to do as the Bible does and sum up counseling discussions in aphoristic form, using the sort of maxim or phrase that is easily learned and retained. Here are a few examples:

> Marriage is a covenant of companionship.
>
> Follow your responsibilities, not your feelings.
>
> Give in to your feelings and you will give up on your responsibilities.
>
> Righteousness simplifies.
>
> Holy living is healthy living.

Such maxims may be used to make teaching portable as well as memorable. Often counselees will write them down on a slip of paper that they place on the refrigerator door, in the car or in a purse. Even if they don't, the maxim is easy to remember. While the counselee may not be able to replicate your full discussion of Genesis 2:18; Proverbs 2:17 and Malachi 2:14, he can easily carry from it the aphorism "Marriage is a covenant of companionship." In the crunch, when faced with temptation or trial, counselees need to be able to center their thinking on succinct statements like that. These bring back the substance of the teaching that was done in more depth. Each of the two words, "covenant" and "companionship," for instance, helps him to recall the two factors significant to marriage: its *nature* as a solemn covenant not to be broken, and its *purpose*, to provide companionship that will dispel the loneliness referred to in Genesis 2:18. The statement, *Follow your responsibilities—no matter how you feel,* and the aphorism, *If you follow your responsibilities, soon right feelings will follow,* help a counselee to pin down those biblical truths. They remind him of what to do when he needs to make decisions on the spot.

When Jesus spoke of cutting off the right hand and foot and plucking out the right eye, he was using shocking, memorable language to teach how to avoid future sin. When he said that one cannot be His disciple unless he hates father, mother, sister, brother and himself, by this striking language He was saying that one must love Him more than anyone else. He used hyperbole. Good counselors use hyperbole all the time (those last three words, you see, are hyperbolic). Hyperbolic language and concepts are striking, as I said. They wake you up; they gain attention and, at first, may even alarm you. They make you think and you easily retain them in your memory,.

When a counselee fails to do an assignment I have given him the previous week, I often shout enthusiastically, "Great! That's just what I've been hoping for," or words to that effect. This regularly startles counselees who sheepishly tell me about it and expect me to jump all over them. Then, having gotten their attention, I explain: "Look, I'm sorry you failed, of course. But if you had to fail, it couldn't have been at a better time. It gives us current data under controlled conditions, the parameters of which I myself set up. So from this failure we can glean data that are from the past week rather than try to dredge up materials from the distant past." Shocking or surprising statements not only get attention and make a deep impression, they may cause counselees to think in ways they may never have thought otherwise.

What I have been trying to say is that rather than the doom-and-gloom sessions that some conduct, a counseling session ought to be vital, informative, memorable, challenging and—at times—even exciting. Teaching and understanding occur most often under such conditions. When a counselee is brought face to face with God in His Word, as I have explained previously, so that he understands that it is God (not merely the counselor) with Whom he is dealing, that makes counseling vital. Nothing you say or do can add to that. But *how* you say and do *what* you say and do may strongly influence whether this encounter takes place or not! Let's look at an example:

Counselor: "So you see, Tom, every passage that we have examined makes it clear that God is requiring you to remain with your wife. I'll grant you that under the circumstances that may be difficult to do, but that's not the issue. God has always called on His children to do difficult things. You know that. And He always provides the strength and the wisdom to accomplish them. Here, in I Corinthians 10:13, He tells you that no trial has come upon you but such as is common to man—God says there that the problem you face is *not unique*. He also says that He will not test you beyond that which you are able to bear—God is saying that your problem is *uniquely fitted* to you. And He says He will make a way out of it so that you will be able to bear it—God promises that eventually, in one way or another, *your problem will be solved.* Do you think that if He sent His Son to die for you to solve your greatest problem, He won't solve this lesser one? How are you going to respond to God? What are you going to say to Him? *That* is the issue."

In counseling, every session should provide an opportunity for the counselee to grow. He grows by learning new truth, determining to apply old truth in new ways, and by actually taking fresh steps forward in his life. Never should a counselee leave a counseling session confused about God's will for his life because your teaching has been unclear. Rarely should he leave without being faced with God in His Word. Often this will come through a fresh understanding of it or through newly-worded ways of teaching new and old things. No person who spoke with Him ever had to leave Jesus the same. If your counselee is brought face to face with Jesus in His Word as you counsel, your counselee need not do so either. In all of this, your use of language is primary.

How is that so? One important fact is the use of the second person. Note in the counselor's comments above how the counselor teaches the counselee *directly* by using the word "you." In explaining the verse from I Corinthians he does so in terms of the counselee himself: "He tells *you*...God says *your* problem...*your* problem...*you* will be able...God says *your* problem..." The verse is treated in a contemporary fashion, as if it were written to the counselee (which, of course, it was. God's Word is for His whole church—of all time). Then he lays it on him, bringing him face to face with God in three pointed questions at the conclusion of his remarks.

You also must learn to adapt your language to those whom you counsel. You counsel persons literate in Christianity and those who are not. There are children and adults—and adults who are childlike in thought and in action, etc. To each, counselors must adapt their language. With young children, for instance, there are times when language must give way to *drawings*. Stick figures (that anyone can draw) are often helpful to represent parents, the child himself and his friends. And *diagrams* similarly are helpful to adults. So supplement language where it may be deficient. But I have noticed that a number of books use diagrams that are so intricate or complex that they confuse rather than clarify. If a diagram doesn't clarify, thus making a truth easier to comprehend, it probably does more harm than good. Diagrams must clarify, not mystify (an aphorism).

In a book, *The Language of Counseling*, I have treated many other aspects of language usage, but by simply mentioning these few I hope to remind you to give careful attention to the ways in which you use language in counseling. After all, as I said at the beginning, it is the counselor's stock-in-trade; it is his bread-and-butter tool. Why not sharpen it and keep it sharp?

Chapter Fourteen

The Use of Antithesis

I cannot stress strongly enough the importance of using biblical antithesis in counseling. Antithesis sharpens issues, brings one to decisions and stresses the absolute nature of God's truth. In short, it focuses one's thinking on how to please God and honor Him. This method of teaching is firmly rooted in the Bible itself. Nothing makes counseling as clear as antithesis. And that is important when people are confused; it tends to cut right through the haze.

The Old Testament speaks of things "clean" and "unclean." This antithetical system of living involved every phase of life from what sort of material one's clothing was made out of (it couldn't be mixed fibers) to the sort of food he ate. Clearly in many of these seemingly arbitrary distinctions God was teaching His people that there were only two ways—His, and all others. It is not that there are several possible options before the believer; no, the option is to please God by doing as He commands or not please Him by doing something—*anything*—else.

The concept of antithesis runs throughout the Bible; Proverbs and the Psalms are full of it. But it is found not only throughout the Old Testament; Jesus spoke of those who were with Him and those who were against Him, He described the narrow way and the broad. He spoke of those who were saved and those who were lost. He taught about eternal life and eternal punishment. New Testament writers contrast light and darkness, truth and error, life and death, the genuine and the false, and so on. The person who immerses himself in the Bible soon develops an antithetical mindset. It is a biblical mindset. Yet so few have it. Rarely do people today—including many well-known Christians—think in antithetical terms. Indeed, many reject it as rigid, legalistic and the like. They are wrong.

Why is that? Of course, the reasons are legion. But, fundamentally, it is true that the average person is constantly bombarded with *continuum* rather than *antithetical* thinking. The schools, the TV, the books and the magazines that one reads all tend to create a non antithetical mindset. Unless one constantly resorts to the Scriptures on a regular basis, he subjects himself to the possibility of being swept away with the continuum thinking of the day. The continuum thinker believes that there is no right or wrong, no true or false. All is relative. There are no absolutes (or if there are, the poles are so far out on the rim of things that they have no effect on thinking or decision making). Since the Bible is explicit about the antithetical nature of the present reality, with the world, the flesh and the devil on the one hand and the church, the Spirit and the Savior on the other, there ought to be no question about how the Christian must align himself. Yet so many Christians do not think antithetically.

Much of the eclecticism that we face in the field of counseling comes from the faulty thinking that is done about this matter. If there is no clear dividing line, then it is OK for Christians to use concepts and methods of counseling that are not a part of a biblical system. In other words, he may borrow from the world. Whenever he does, however, he ends up thinking and acting unbiblically. His counsel and his teaching are adversely affected. At length he will find himself contradicting what the Bible says. Ultimately, non-antithetical thinking drifts into error. He may rationalize his position so as to "fit" it into what the Scriptures teach. But, either way, in the end he will teach that which the Scriptures do not. And that can be serious in the lives of those whom he counsels. Is your thinking ordered into antithetical categories?

It is true that *within* the biblical parameters set up by God there is often room for either/or decision making. God is the God of abundance; often He offers options. But, when suggesting options, the counselor must be absolutely sure that these are options that lie firmly within the parameters of Scripture. He may not offer any options that do not. Marriage to either one of two different potential Christian husbands may be a legitimate option; it is no option to marry a third who is not a Christian.

When setting forth the options with which one is faced, again it is important to set them out as God's options—not as your own. You never have the right to determine what another person may or may not do. You must be able to show unmistakably that the options that you reject as well as those that you hold out are truly biblical. Let's consider a case or two.

A Christian is trying to decide whether or not to go into a certain business. The company that has invited him to take over the management of its southern region has stipulated that he must put the company first—before family or anything else. May he take the job? That is his question. The answer is that if the company persists in demanding his *first* loyalty, he may not. The Bible, in the order of concern in Ephesians 5 and 6, as well as in the order of creation, etc., puts the husband's wife and family on a higher plane than work. So, unless he can persuade the company that he can do a better job by conforming to the biblical standard, he will find it necessary to turn down the offer, regardless of how lucrative it may be. Many men would reason, "Well, to take this job would mean so much more money that I can provide for my family; so I *am* putting them first." That is pure rationalization. One who thinks this way wants to erase the antithesis. He will soon find himself doing so in many other ways, once he has made this basic error of judgment against what he knows to be God's intention for him.

So long as the antithesis between God's ways and all others remains sharp and clear, one's counseling is not likely to stray

too far from the truth. It is when he attempts to fuzz up the dividing line that trouble begins. To knock down partitions that God
Himself erected is to court danger. And it is to misrepresent
God's will. Some will do so out of fear of consequences—after
all, they might be called "rigid" by those who think that the biblical antitheses fail to allow enough freedom of movement. So,
with the idea that they know better than God, they push the line a
little to the right or to the left. But, in the long run, though at the
time it may not seem so, God's way always proves to be the
more generous, more compassionate, freer way. You can't out-
guess God.

Antithesis is what makes an approach truly Christian—not
antithesis itself, but the antithesis of that which is biblical toward
that which is not. If there is a God and He has given "all things
pertaining to life and godliness" in His Word (II Peter 1:3), then
anything that is other than that should be set over against it as
opposing it.

When Jesus said, "Whoever isn't with Me is against Me, and
whoever doesn't gather with Me scatters" (Matthew 12:30), He
was setting forth the antithesis. In that aphorism He was speaking of the unbeliever. Those who are not actively allied with Him
by saving faith, working for Him, are *against* Him and *working*
against Him (scattering). That statement is a clear and plain
statement of the antithesis. Some who read this will immediately
counter with Mark 9:40, "Anybody who isn't against us is for
us." How may the seeming contradiction in the two passages be
reconciled? Simply by observing that in the Mark context (vv.
38-41) it is clear that though the one who was casting out
demons was not part of the twelve, he was a disciple of Christ.
What he did, he did *in His Name* (vv. 38,39,41). Those mentioned in Matthew were unbelievers, *scattering* the work of
Christ, thus working *against* Him; the other was *doing* the work
of Christ, thus *gathering* with Him. There is no antithesis among
believers; the antithesis is between believers and unbelievers,

between God's ways and ungodly ways. The Psalms, in particular, from the first Psalm on, set up the antithesis between the two ways and the two kinds of people who walk on them. It is not right for Christians, therefore, to become enamored with the ways of the world. From the garden of Eden, it has always been a choice between God's Word and the devil's, between the way of life and the way of death. Christian counselors recognize the antithesis, and counsel accordingly. Except within the parameters given in the Scripture, in which God Himself gives options, the counselor should take the stance and use the language of antithesis, sharply setting forth the two ways—even as the Psalmist and the Lord Jesus Christ did. He has no right to dull or obscure that which God has set forth so sharply. Where God has spoken antithetically, he dare not speak otherwise. Indeed, the whole matter of whether one will counsel using antithesis is a matter of antithesis. There are only two ways to counsel—God's way and all others. And God's way is the antithetical way.

Chapter Fifteen

Techniques of Teaching

Techniques are important. Jesus, the prophets and the apostles used various techniques to get their message across. Good teachers have available at all times a variety of techniques that they may use when needed. Poor teachers seldom vary their techniques. That is one reason why they are poor teachers.

In His teaching Jesus used parables, repetition, questioning, argument, examples, illustrations, object lessons, etc. If you are unfamiliar with anything other than mere conversational teaching in counseling, it is time for you to increase your repertoire. Certain techniques are appropriate on occasions when others are not. Some are more helpful in one context than others. It is the sorting out of some of these (I cannot be exhaustive) that I wish to do in this chapter to give you a "feel" of how one may best use which techniques when counseling.

Obviously there is the bread-and-butter technique of didactic teaching, in which one simply sets forth in plain (though colorful and vibrant), unmistakable language that which the counselee needs to know. But what if he tends to be forgetful? What if he treats your teaching as ho hum material? What if he has a hard time accepting things he doesn't want to hear? What if he is inept at listening or always seems to distrust what you say? What if...(you fill in the rest)? Then you need to use a different approach.

How about using a parable? A parable is a story that you place over against a truth you wish to get across. It has a brief introduction, a complication, usually suspense and a climax (sometimes followed by a conclusion). A parable, which is taken from life around you, has a twist or a surprise that causes one to think. Take the three-part parable of Luke 15 in which after gaining assent from the listener that shepherds, women and fathers rejoice (along with the angels) when that which was lost is found, Jesus then switches to the elder brother who is out of sync with the rest. He is like the Pharisees who grumbled at Christ's seeking the lost by eating with them. The twist, or kicker, at the end is the surprise element that gives the parable its force. It is the point of the parable. The listener is there assenting to the first part, the second and finally to the third, when suddenly the twist comes and the parable takes a new turn that is totally at odds with everything you have assented to. You in effect are saying, "Yes, yes, yes—*what*?"

Well, that is one of Christ's well-known parables. Why don't you try to compose four or five for situations in which you had a counselee who was reluctant to do what God says about one matter or another? Here are a couple of situations to get you started:

1. You have been telling a counselee about the fact that God has an answer even to *his* problem. He is doubtful. You need to stress the fact. So you tell him the following parable:

2. A counselee argues that it is always possible to refuse to be reconciled with someone who has wronged him, though he is willing to forgive him. You want to show him that forgiveness means he can no longer use the sin

against the offender and that reconciliation is necessary. So you tell him the following parable:

Do you get the idea? You say, "It's hard to make up a parable." Yes! It is. And it is therefore important to take time to do so whenever you are stumped for a way of making a point clear to a counselee. Rarely, because you are not Jesus Christ, will you find yourself composing and using parables on the spot. They will take thought and time to produce. But once you have done so, perhaps even after the occasions on which they would have been helpful, they, nevertheless, will be usable many other times in the future. And, as Jesus often did, you may frequently use the basic format with variations on the theme.

Parables are but one way of awakening counselees to truth and helping them to remember what they have learned. All that I have to do to help you recall an entire parable with the impact of its message, for instance, is to say "The Good Samaritan." It all comes back—doesn't it? So use parables not only to make a point, but also to help counselees remember that point later on when you may need once again to refer to the truth that it teaches.

In His teaching, Jesus also referred to recent incidents. He spoke of the tower that fell on those who had been killed (Luke 13:4) and of Zechariah who was murdered between the temple and the altar (Matthew 23:35). Some of the most powerful illustrations in counseling come from the daily newspaper. Read it each day. Think of some event that may pertain to a situation that is apropos to a counselee, have it in hand to use and then power-fully do so. "You know what happened in the trial that is all over the newspapers, don't you? Today they let the murderer off on a technicality. Everyone knows that he is guilty; he was caught red handed. He may get away for now; he won't for eternity. If you think God will let you off on the technicality that you have raised, forget it. He won't! I'm not here to read you your 'rights.' You have none before God. He doesn't submit to the Miranda act. You are guilty. You know it, I know it and God knows it. You can get nowhere with God by throwing up technicalities. He's not concerned about technicalities; He's concerned with justice. He won't let you off."

Repetition also is important. I have mentioned this previ-ously, but I want to enlarge on it here. A key word or phrase (perhaps one of your aphorisms) repeated throughout the session 6 - 8 - 10 times tends to stick in the memory of the counselee. For instance, if you are emphasizing the idea that he must study his Bible every day, you might say, "Now, Brent, I want you to know that every day you should read and pray. And every day when you read and pray, you can expect so and so to happen. But if you fail every day to read and pray, then you can expect such and such." Perhaps that is a bit compressed, but it gives you the idea. The rhyming words *every day* and *read and pray* are used over and over again until he gets the point.

The use of printed materials has been mentioned. Let me add to that the use of videos to illustrate a point. Having a VCR in the counseling room for such purposes is useful. Moreover, there are times to play audio tapes as well. And it is not unusual for the better counselors to use a chalk board or white board as well. Charts, brochures on pertinent subjects, materials prewritten and published (at least by desktop publishing) are all vital to good counseling. As they develop, handing out computer programs will become a wave of the future. It would be useful for some Christian computer programmer to develop some software that could be used as training in basic Christian living skills which many counselees need to learn. But that is all in the offing.

Role playing is, perhaps, the most dramatic teaching technique you will use. I have described the values of role playing in the introduction to *The Christian Counselor's Casebook*, so I shall not repeat that material here. In order to discover whether a counselee has fully understood and is well-enough prepared to carry out a vital assignment (particularly when it involves confronting another), role play it.

> *Counselor*: "Let me see how you will approach Ed and just what you will say to him. I'll play the part of Ed; go ahead..."

If he does well, you can have confidence he will pull it off. If, on the other hand, he does poorly, you will need to practice it again—and again, and again—till he gets it right. If necessary, you may need to switch roles and show him how to do and say what he must. Recently I did that very thing when teaching someone how to approach a prospect.

If role play is the most dramatic teaching technique, then possibly monitoring is the most direct. In monitoring, the counselor persuades someone else (husband, wife, parent, friend) to monitor the progress of the counselee during the week, especially concentrating on critical episodes. The monitor not only reports at the next session what he has observed, but during the week reminds, coaches and otherwise helps the counselee to fulfil his assignments. It is important to obtain the counselee's agreement to use a monitor. This is a very effective method of helping the counselee to succeed. It is frequently used in the early sessions. But, in using this method, be sure to adequately instruct the monitor in detail.

The principle here is that the biblical teachers used all sorts of materials. You too should do so. You, yourself, could probably add some ideas to those mentioned in this chapter. Why not go ahead and do so. The idea here is to get you thinking about the matter, not to supply everything for you. I hope that you have been stimulated to add your own notes to the margins of these pages. As you read, ideas may pop up in your thinking. As they do, jot them down. I hope you learn to do that with all the reading you do. But, in particular, I would be delighted if you were stimulated by this book to do so in every chapter. In that way, the book could become a personalized treatise to which you could return for help many times in the future.

Chapter Sixteen

What Does a Counselor Teach?

There are so many areas about which counselors will find it necessary to teach their counselees that it is impossible to mention them all. They must be able, as I have been saying throughout, to teach "the whole counsel of God." Rather than treat a few of these areas in depth to attempt to be exhaustive, therefore, in this chapter I shall mention a few of the major areas that, by the sheer frequency of the need, *demand* teaching on the part of the counselor. In each area, I shall consider but one or two points that—out of all that may be said about it—*must* be said. In other books, especially in the reference volumes *The Christian Counselor's Manual* and *The Theology of Counseling,* I have treated other material thoroughly. I do not wish to replicate that material here.

Marriage Problems

Every sort of difficulty that you can think of—and more—may occur. But out of them all, possibly the most important consideration is the lack of teaching (*true biblical* teaching) about love. Apropos this matter, the observant counselor will discover that two facts need to be taught:

1. Love is an *obligation* of marriage, not a *basis* for marriage. Tell counselees this fact over and over again. Because of the many forces that teach otherwise they will have a hard time understanding and believing this

fact. Most Americans, it seems, have a totally romantic view of love—if they have any sort of view at all. TV and Hollywood have played a major role in fostering this false view. Because of this ethos of our times, many marriages—even Christian marriages—are in jeopardy.

In the history of the world, many (if not most) marriages have been arranged by others (parents, matchmakers, etc.). They have not been based on love. These have not proven less successful than romantically-based marriages. While we don't necessarily want to go back to arranged marriages, it would be wise to have possible marriage alliances more carefully scrutinized and approved by Christian parents and the church. Given biblical commitment on all sides, even an arranged marriage can be highly successful. That is because, essentially, marriage is *covenantal* (cf. Proverbs 2:17; Malachi 2:14); it involves a *commitment* of two persons to provide mutual *companionship* (see the two verses just mentioned). Most traditional marriage vows, you will notice, have it right: in the ceremony the two parties *obligate* themselves to love one another. Love is not the basis for marriage; it is an obligation of marriage.

2. Love is not primarily a feeling. Love is, first of all, giving. It involves giving to one's partner (out of what one has) that which the other needs. Note the operative verb in John 3:16, Ephesians 5:25, Galatians 2:20, Romans 12:20 is *give*. When one gives his time, money, interest, ability, effort fully enough and long enough, his feelings will come into line. But he does not have to feel like doing so in order to obey God by giving himself and his interest to his marriage partner. Love, then, is not feeling first; it is giving first—feelings follow. Incidentally, another fact closely connected with this one is the biblical insight that love is principally the obligation of the

husband. That, of course, is because the husband is to be to his wife what Christ is to His bride the church (see Ephesians 5). It was Christ, not the church, Who first loved and Who, by His Spirit, maintains love in the ranks. For help on this and other matters, see my *Christian Living in the Home*.

Sexual Problems

Ordinarily what needs to be *taught* is not biological facts (these can easily be supplied by handing out appropriate literature) but the spiritual facts pertaining to sex. Paul writes "The wife doesn't have authority over her own body; rather it is her husband who does. Also, the husband doesn't have authority over his own body; rather it is his wife who does" (I Corinthians 7:4). These words are virtually unknown, yet they are altogether important. Not only do they forbid autoeroticism but, of even greater import, they direct both the husband and the wife alike to follow the fundamental principle regarding proper sexual relations.

Paul is explicit: neither the husband nor the wife has authority (or rights) over his/her body. Those rights belong to one's spouse. Get that across to counselees. It will be a new thought to many, if not most of them. But what does Paul mean? First, that there is no need for either to get himself/herself "up" for sexual intercourse. Rather it is the obligation of each to prepare his/her partner for the act. Self-stimulation, trying to "psych" one's self up for sexual relations, and the like, are wrong. One's only task is to *give* in love. In this context, that means he/she thinks not of self but of the other. He/she prepares the other by stimulating his/her body in preparation for the sexual act. Love focuses on the other person, not on one's self.

Secondly, under this biblical arrangement there never is a possibility of one partner demanding something of the other that is abhorrent. Neither has authority over his body so as to demand anything. Conversely, together, each tries to satisfy the other; not himself. Therefore when one or the other complains in counseling that "She [he] doesn't satisfy me," a biblical counselor will respond by saying something like this: "That's hardly the issue, is it? The real question is 'Are you satisfying your partner?'" He will then read and explain this verse, in response to the amazed replies that he usually receives at this point. This fundamental principle, known by so few, will help couples immensely once they get a grasp on it and put it into practice as the guideline for all their sexual activity. It is the principle of love shown by giving in sexual relations. Following it will eliminate most sexual difficulties you encounter.

Forgiveness

Forgiveness is the oil that keeps homes, churches and groups of all sorts running smoothly. Human beings since Adam—with only one exception—sin against each other. It is inevitable that sinners will do so. That is why forgiveness is needed. I am speaking here not about forgiveness by God but between the brothers of the Church. Forgiveness is needed; where it is absent, Christians end up in the counseling room.

Since, as Ephesians 4:32 says, our forgiveness must be modeled after God's forgiveness of us in Christ, we must ask "What does God do when He forgives?" The answer is that He goes on record saying, "I will remember your sins no more" (Isaiah 43:25; see also 44:22). God, of course, forgets nothing. But forgetting and not remembering are two different things. Forgetting is passive; it is just something that human beings do (they can't control it). Not remembering, however, is active; it is possible not to bring up (that is what "remember" in Isaiah, III John 10, etc. means) a matter. God means that he will not bring up and use their sins against them in the future. So when you say, "I forgive you," you are promising another not to bring up his sin to him, to others or to yourself in the future; you are burying it. You will not use it against him. Most counselees must be taught this all-important understanding of forgiveness.

The second factor is that a counselee must refuse to hold bitterness against anyone (Ephesians 4:31,32), and must always be ready to forgive another when he says that he repents (cf. Luke 17:3ff). Counselees, however, must be taught to *grant* forgiveness (i.e., make the promise not to remember) *only after another has said that he is wrong (repented) and seeks forgiveness.* God does not forgive anyone apart from repentance—otherwise all would be saved. He forgives only those who repent of their sin and trust the Savior. For you to forgive another who will not repent (as some erroneously teach that you should) would bring about a situation in which you could not obey Matthew 18:15ff. But God's commandments never place you in such a dilemma.

And it is of critical importance in this day of self-centeredness to understand the purpose of forgiveness. Forgiveness is primarily for the sake of the offender and, secondarily, to reestablish proper relationships; only as a by-product does it benefit the one who forgives. This emphasis is turned around in almost every present-day volume on forgiveness; the only concern is for the one who forgives. This emphasis on self must be countered by biblical teaching. All sorts of self-focused counselors advise forgiving others whether they know about it or not! The only thing that matters is the forgiver's welfare (feelings). Love impels us, like God, to do all we can to bring the wrongdoer to repentance and reconciliation—*for his sake.*

Depression

Depression is one of the most common complaints (often in addition to other problems) you will meet in counseling. You must, first of all, distinguish true depression from a different, minor problem that many *call* depression. True depression is not "feeling down, feeling blue." Everyone, it seems, from time to time, for a variety of reasons, has days like that. True depression is *giving up*. It is a condition in which one has given up on his responsibilities, on his family and friends, his interests and hobbies—perhaps even on life. He has ceased functioning. A truly depressed person's speech is filled with the word "can't" ("I can't go on; I can't take it any more"). He is in despair; he says such things as, "What's the use of trying? Why go on? The situation is hopeless. Others would be better off without me."

Depression is caused by giving up on one's responsibilities when, for whatever reason, he is in a "down period." He has given in to feelings and, consequently, has given up on his responsibilities. To *avoid* depression, when a counselee feels like quitting, he must not. He should be taught the facts found in II Corinthians 4:8,9 and also verse 1. Here it is evident that Paul had every reason to feel like giving up, but he refused to follow those feelings. To see how he was afflicted, read Chapters 6 and 11 in this same epistle. If anyone ever faced circumstances that might encourage him to throw in the towel, it was Paul. Why didn't he? II Corinthians 4:1 makes it clear: "Therefore, since we have this service to perform as the result of mercy, we don't give up." Gratitude toward God for what He had done in saving and giving him responsibilities impelled Paul forward. He did not chuck his responsibilities when he felt like doing so. In the midst of perplexity and trouble untold, he remembered the mercy of God that saved and commissioned him, and went on. If, out of gratitude toward God for His great salvation, a counselee perseveres, he too will avoid depression. Gratitude drives one through times of difficulty.

How does a counselee extricate himself from depression? Repenting of his sin, he must reassume his responsibilities, remembering God's goodness to Him in Christ. If his thinking needs to be refreshed about God's love in Christ, tell him to reread the four passion narratives. He does not have to feel like reassuming his responsibilities; he probably won't. He just has to *do* it—because he wants to please God. If he does so out of gratitude and perseveres, he will quickly emerge from depression and will be able to avoid it in the future.

Money

Money is *not* "the root of all evil," as many misquote the Bible verse. The Scriptures call "the *love* of money *a* root of all sorts of evil" (I Timothy 6:10). Indeed, in discussing riches in this very passage, Paul says that "God richly provides everything for our enjoyment" (v. 17). Then why is there so much trouble over money? What must counselors teach about money? Counselors need to make it clear to counselees that to *love* (not to have or to use) money is sin. One must love God and his neighbor. If he does, he will not love money; if he loves money, to the extent that he does, he will fail to love God and neighbor.

So the answer to the problem of money-loving is to help the counselee change his goal of life, reorienting himself toward the love of God and others instead. Those who "determine to be rich" (I Timothy 6:9) who are "eager for money" (v. 10) must alter everything. Otherwise their lives will be filled with sorrow and disappointment. In doing so, they must substitute proper interests and activities for those excessively spent in procuring money. These simple but all-important facts are precisely what some counselees need to be taught. In order to do so, it is important to do a full exposition of all that I Timothy 6 has to say and be ready to express every aspect of it. You should be ready at all times to teach from this *locus classicus* on the subject.

The Tongue

Both James and the Book of Proverbs make it clear how speech—that blessing with which God endowed the human race—can become a curse to one's self and to others rather than a blessing. Gossip, speaking negatively about others, harsh replies—all of these and many other offenses of the tongue bring heartache and conflict. If "no human being anywhere is able to tame the tongue" (James 3:8), what hope is there for your counselees? How can you help them? By remembering that nothing is impossible with *God*. What man can't do, God can. By regular, prayerful practice of the principles of Scripture concerning speech, it can be made a blessing once more (cf. Romans 12:14). The counselee must learn to "bless" others with his speech. He must be taught to count to ten when angry (Proverbs 17:27), to work at giving a "soft answer" (Proverbs 15:1) and to offer constructive words that will build up another by solving problems rather than intensifying them through destructive words (Ephesians 4:29). Many verses in chapters 10 and 18 of Proverbs, in addition to other verses throughout the book of Proverbs, tell what the counselor needs to know about the use of speech.

Conflict

In Romans 12:18 Paul urges, "If possible, so far as it depends on you, be at peace with everybody." That should be the objective that you set before your counselees. It is a realistic statement that says, in effect, if there is going to be conflict, be sure that it isn't because you started or continued it. Many counselees like to keep a conflict going, even if they didn't start it. Jesus taught, "Happy are the peacemakers, since they will be called God's sons" (Matthew 5:9). In II Thessalonians 3:12, Paul sets forth the goal of working with "quietness," an aspiration that reflects the fuller statement of I Thessalonians 4:11: "Eagerly aspire to live a quiet life." That sort of life seems far too tame for some. The reason is that they think that the only excitement in this world comes from conflict (they have been trained to think this way by sports, newspapers, TV newscasts, talk radio and movies which thrive on it). True, lasting excitement, however, is found in pursuing the work of the Lord with zeal. Colossians 3:15 does not speak of peace within but peace among the members of the body, which is achieved by pursuing those things mentioned in Colossians 3:12,13. Self-seeking causes conflict, as James points out (James 4:1ff.; on this verse, see *The Christian Counselor's Commentary* on James). Seeking the welfare of others rather than one's own quells conflict (Philippians 2:2-4). Adding fuel to the fire intensifies conflict (cf. Proverbs 17:14; 15:18) and pride always leads to contention (Proverbs 13:10). Set forth the principles of Romans 12:14ff. concretely for counselees as the means for combating aggression and conflict, weaving some of the verses mentioned above into the discussion as a groundwork for change.

Fear

When angels appear, one of the first words they speak is "fear not." Why? When sinful people encounter God—or even His messengers—they recognize their sin and are afraid (cf. I Corinthians 15:54-57; Isaiah 6). "The fear of the Lord is the beginning of wisdom." To fear God, as one ought to, is to cast aside all other fears. Jesus said, "Don't be afraid of those who kill the body but can't kill the soul; rather be afraid of the One Who can destroy both soul and body in Gehenna" (Matthew 10:28). In I John 4:18 the same point is made this way: "There is no fear in love; rather, love that has accomplished its purpose throws fear out." Love is the only power greater than fear. When one truly loves God and his neighbor enough to *give* himself for them, fear is cast out. Seek commitment from counselees to assume the loving responsibilities that they have abandoned out of fear, no matter what the consequences may be. To overcome fear, foster love. Biblical study of Christ's love engenders love in the counselee (I John 4:19).

Commitment

Commitment involves at least five things. These need to be explained to counselees before calling for commitment from them. They are:

1. An understanding of that to which one is committing himself.
2. A desire to do it (not necessarily the act itself, but to do it out of a desire to please God, even when that act is displeasing to one's self).
3. Ability, skills and resources to pull it off (or a willingness to acquire these if necessary).
4. A concrete plan for achieving the end desired, together with a schedule for accomplishing the task.
5. Follow through of the sort that *does* all that is planned, according to schedule.

Because most people talk about commitment, but never take the time or give the thought to define and teach it, much commitment (which is not true commitment at all) fails. It is important for every counselor prior to commitment to review what is involved and to make sure that there is commitment of the sort outlined above.

Guidance

Many books on guidance misguide. Such things as open doors, circumstances, putting out the fleece, promptings, feeling led, looking for signs, trying to interpret dreams, and listening for God to answer in prayer are all wrong ways of seeking God's guidance. That is not the way to discern His will. There is no biblical basis for adopting any of these methods which, if followed, are likely to lead to frustration and failure. Counselors themselves must be clear about the matter and must be able to help counselees to avoid these traps.

Even Paul did not enter every *open door* (cf. II Corinthians 3:12,13). Open doors sometimes lead to elevator shafts. And, unlike sardine cans, *circumstances* do not come with a key attached. Your counselee brings his own interpretation to the circumstance. He applies for a visa to India. It is denied. How shall he interpret it? He may conclude, "The Lord doesn't want me to be a missionary." Or, he may think, "He wants me to be a missionary somewhere else." Or perhaps he says, "Well, the Lord is testing me; I'll go to India if I have to swim." Which will it be?

Gideon's *fleece* was a special case in which God "put up with" his asking for a sign. Gideon himself acknowledged that it was wrong, asking the Lord not to be angry with him (Judges 6:39). Incidentally, how many times does the coin have to land face up? No, Jesus said "an evil and adulterous generation seeks a *sign.*"

There is absolutely nothing in Scripture about *"feeling* led" or receiving *"promptings* and *checks* in the *spirit."* And how utterly important it is to emphasize that *prayer* is talking to God; there is no promise that He will talk to you in prayer. God speaks through the Bible; we speak to Him through prayer.

In all of these attempts to discern God's will in particular situations the person involved wants God to make his decisions for him. There is no promise that He will do so. God will not do the counselee's work for him. The Bible, it is true, has some specific statements about God's will ("You may not commit adultery"), but for the most part, provides only general principles. These principles form parameters within which God expects the counselee himself to make decisions. One reason for much error is the notion that if one misses "God's perfect will," he will be stuck with something lesser. There is no such concept in the Bible. Turning to any other source than the Bible—or to those resources and resource persons that can help you understand biblical teaching—is to court danger. Teach counselees about this. Many need to hear. Some may have initiated their problems by following faulty means of guidance. Check for this possibility; the problem is rife—far more frequent, I am beginning to realize, than at first I had supposed.

Worry

I have written extensively about worry elsewhere, developing Matthew 6 and Philippians 4. Here I wish to emphasize but one point. I have discovered that Christians who are ashamed to admit many other failures in their lives readily confess to being worriers—and even laugh or joke about it! That is because worry is the respectable sin. Sin—that is the important word in the last sentence. That worry is sin is what you must teach counselees; they don't know that. Until they see it as sin, they will not be motivated sufficiently to change; counselees must be made to take the sin of worry seriously.

How do we know that worry is sin? Well, what is sin? It is doing what God forbids or failing to do what He requires. Worry is a sin on both counts. In Philippians 4, God forbids worry about "anything" and "in everything" requires prayer instead. Those two words are absolutes. There never is a time or a circumstance in which worry is not sinful. To disobey either command is sin. Worry is not respectable because, as Jesus clearly points out in Matthew 6, it is distrust in the care of a loving, heavenly Father.

Idolatry

Anything may become an idol by attributing to it the devotion and attachment that is due God. For instance, Paul writes that "greed is idolatry" (Colossians 3:5). Whatever one desires so much that it consumes his time, thought and other interests, he has made an idol. Counselors may not look into hearts to determine what counselees think, desire, etc., but they may warn them about idolatry, instructing them that it is possible to make idols of people, possessions or positions.

Many counselees come so strongly focused on obtaining some object that it soon becomes apparent that they must be faced with the possibility that they have made it an idol. Whenever any counselee so strongly desires anything other than to please God that he is dominated by it, you must point out the dangers of idolatry. Contrary to what some think, Christians can become idolatrous. That is why John issues his strong warning, "Dear children, guard yourselves from idols" (I John 5:21). How does one do so? By putting to death "the habits of the members of" one's body (see Colossians 3:5). For help on this, see my book *Winning The War Within*. The goal is to replace the old idolatrous desires with new righteous ones. *The issue boils down to this: what does the counselee want most?*

There are other areas about which I might say many things, but actually, if one understands and operates clearly with these key items, with these key areas in mind, he will dispel much of the difficulty that now abounds in counseling circles.

Conclusion

Well, there you have it. Obviously much more might be said about many things, but the combination of principles and practices set forth here is designed to meet the need for a semester's introductory course on the process of teaching in counseling. Doubtless few such courses now exist, if any, but perhaps this book will be the inspiration for such a course. It is also intended to benefit the counselor who has never thought through many of these matters, and wants to do so. Finally, those who are now undertaking counseling for the first time will find the book helpful as a challenge to begin counseling with a proper perspective on the matter of teaching—something that all too few have been encouraged to do.

It is my hope that in reading you have seen three things in the process: 1) that teaching plays a large, integral role in effective biblical counseling; 2) that there is a necessary correspondence between beliefs and practices; 3) that the Bible not only must provide the materials for both, but is entirely sufficient to do so.

Teaching is for all Christians as counseling is for all Christians—informally. But teaching is for the few as counseling is for the few—officially. Informal, occasional counseling fits the biblical pattern. This book, I hope, will be an aid to all who seek to fulfill this biblical mandate. But those engaged in official counseling and, therefore, teaching as a life calling, will also profit from the volume. Perhaps many questions will be raised among the latter for which I have provided but the merest hints and answers, or only minimal replies. I trust that some will be encouraged by this book to explore these aspects of teaching in counseling to develop more detailed responses to those questions and that they will publish their findings.

Two major thrusts of this book have been to stress the importance of teaching in the work of counseling and the concomitant care with which one must carry on such teaching. The prime concern behind these thrusts is love for God and one's neighbor, the counselee. Care is called for because God's will, found in His Word, must not be misread, misunderstood or misrepresented. To attribute teaching to God that is not His is the grave danger to be avoided. The danger arises from representing God as something that He is not, thereby teaching harmful error to counselees at a vulnerable time in their lives.

Throughout, while encouraging genuine concern for counselees, I have subordinated that concern to the counselor's concern to please and glorify God. The work of teaching in counseling is peculiarly His work. The Christian counselor counsels not in his own name, but as a "man from God" (II Timothy 3:17). He stands in the breach between the counselee and God and between the counselee and his neighbor, in the Name of Christ seeking to bring about reconciliation, harmony and understanding through the power of the Spirit, manifested in His ministered Word. No wonder James warned about taking up this work too quickly as so many, failing to heed his warning—for whatever reason—have done. Perhaps one of the salutary effects of this book will be to awaken the consciences of such persons to the need either to take the work more seriously, get proper training and counsel as they ought, or to back off entirely from official counseling. I would be gratified if the book challenged some who should to take up the work, provided they do so with all the seriousness and effort required. And I would be more than satisfied if the only result of the publication of this volume was that some who have been reluctant to teach counselees boldly begin to do so with clarity.

Truth, life and ministry are what the biblical counselor-teacher works with: all three in balance. The ministry (service) of God and neighbor in which one engages when doing so will be effective only to the extent that he develops the lifestyle requisite to it. On the other hand, the lifestyle he needs properly develops only in relationship to the truth that he assimilates. Each is dependent on the other; a counselor, therefore, must excel in all three. To neglect any one is to neglect all.

The work of counseling is a humbling task. Again and again, as a counselor deals with counselees, he recognizes the depths of human sin and sees in them his own foibles. But it is also a glorious calling (II Corinthians 3). Those whom God has called to the work are privileged to labor in the study, acquisition and ministry of Scripture—a wonderful and blessed work. In gratitude, then, with the apostle Paul, in times of discouragement and doubt, let us say,

> since we have this service to perform as the result of mercy, we don't give up.   (II Corinthians 4:1)

Counselor-teacher, take heart!

Other Titles by Dr. Jay Adams

available from your bookstore or
directly from TIMELESS TEXTS
1-800-814-1045

What to do on Thursday—A Layman's Guide to the Practical Use of the Scriptures
by Jay E. Adams   144pp. paperback

> The Bible has the answers, but can you find, understand and apply them?
> *What to do on Thursday* teaches you how to study and interpret your Bible
> to answer the questions that arise all week at work, at play, at home, and at
> school.

> Dr. Adams has written this study to prepare you to meet the challenges of
> this fast-moving world with decisions that will honor God. The practical use
> of the Scriptures on an everyday basis is crucial to all of God's people. You
> can't wait for your pastor to preach a sermon that applies to your need now.
> *What to do on Thursday* will help you prepare a template of priorities that
> will order your life in a Godly pattern.

The Grand Demonstration—A Biblical Study of the So-Called Problem of Evil
by Jay E. Adams   119pp. paperback

> Why is there sin, rape, disease, war, pain and death in a good God's world?
> Every Christian asks this question—but rarely receives an answer. Read this
> book and discover what God Himself says.

> *The Grand Demonstration* penetrates deeply into scriptural teaching regard-
> ing the nature of God. Moving into territory others fear to tread, Dr. Adams
> maintains that a fearless acceptance of biblical truth solves the so-called
> "problem of evil".

(Winning) the War Within—A Biblical Strategy for Spiritual Warfare
by Jay E. Adams   151pp. paperback

> Christian, you are at war! It is the battles at two levels—one outward, the
> other inward—that are our responsibilities as members of the church. While
> the outer battle is vital and pressing, it cannot be fought as it should be
> unless the Christian is successfully winning the war *within*. Do you know
> how to fight the war within? This book—reflecting the spirit of the Word of
> God—has been written to tell you in no uncertain terms that there is a way
> to victory. And, avoiding the path of mere theory, it explains how you, no
> matter how many times you have been defeated in the past, can begin to con-
> sistently win the battles within.

A Thirst For Wholeness
by Jay E. Adams   143pp. paperback

How healthy is your spiritual integrity? Do your actions speak so loudly that
people won't listen? *A Thirst for Wholeness* provides the solution to this
common problem. Drawing on the book of James, Dr. Adams concentrates
on how you can become a complete Christian from the inside out. As you
study the inner dynamics involved in this process, you'll learn how to get
your spiritual beliefs and your everyday actions in sync.

Truth Applied—Application in Preaching
by Jay E. Adams   144pp. paperback

Too often, a sermon founders on a preacher's failure to make a good connec-
tion between a message originally delivered to God's people millennia ago
and the congregation in the here and now. Dr. Adams has long been concerned for the art and science and passion of preaching. In this book he
offers a cogent, biblical philosophy of application, together with practical
suggestions about how the busy preacher can readily implement it.

The Christian Counselor's Commentary Series
by Jay E. Adams   all volumes hardback

Vol. 1—I & II Corinthians
Vol. 2—Galatians, Ephesians, Colossians & Philemon
Vol. 3—I & II Timothy and Titus
Vol. 4—Romans, Philippians, and I & II Thessalonians

This series of commentaries is written in everyday English. A must for the
layman as well as the Pastor/Counselor. Dr. Adams' everyman style of communication brings forth these biblical truths in a clear understandable way
that typifies his writings. He does not try to duplicate the standard, more
technical types of commentaries but supplements them with the implications
of the text for God-honoring counseling and Christian living.

The Christian Counselor's New Testament
translated by Jay E. Adams   leather & synthetic bindings

A special translation by Dr. Adams with extensive footnotes and topical side
columns. This Bible was specially designed to help the Christian in study as
well as counseling. *The Christian Counselor's New Testament* is very user
friendly. It leads you through those tough counseling topics by using the
Margin Notations and Notation Index for the topic or related topics. Easily
used during the counseling session.